Controlling Corruption in Europe
The Anticorruption Report
Volume 1

Alina Mungiu-Pippidi (editor)

Controlling Corruption in Europe

The Anticorruption Report 1

written by
Alina Mungiu-Pippidi
Roxana Bratu
Nicholas Charron
Valentina Dimulescu
Madalina Doroftei
Mihály Fazekas
Aare Kasemets
Lawrence Peter King
Roberto Martínez B. Kukutschka
Raluca Pop
István János Tóth

Barbara Budrich Publishers
Opladen • Berlin • Toronto 2013

A CIP catalogue record for this book is available from
Die Deutsche Bibliothek (The German Library)

© 2013 by Barbara Budrich Publishers, Opladen, Berlin & Toronto
www.barbara-budrich.net

ISBN   978-3-8474-0125-4 (Paperback)
eISBN   978-3-8474-0381-4 (e-book)

Die Deutsche Bibliothek – CIP-Einheitsaufnahme
Ein Titeldatensatz für die Publikation ist bei Der Deutschen Bibliothek erhältlich.

Verlag Barbara Budrich Barbara Budrich Publishers
Stauffenbergstr. 7. D-51379 Leverkusen Opladen, Germany

86 Delma Drive. Toronto, ON M8W 4P6 Canada
www.barbara-budrich.net

Jacket illustration by Bettina Lehfeldt, Kleinmachnow, Germany –
www.lehfeldtgraphic.de
Printed in Germany on acid-free paper by
Strauss GmbH, Mörlenbach, Germany

Contents

Executive summary 7

1. Methodology 9
2. European Union Member States. 14
3. The South-Eastern Europe. 48
4. The Former Soviet Union 55
5. Top of the Class. The Case of Estonia 68
6. Hidden Depths. The Case of Hungary 74
7. Bottom of the Heap. The Case of Romania 83
8. European Perceptions of Quality
   of Government: A Survey of 24 Countries 99
9. Lessons Learned. The Good, the Bad and the Ugly 121

Acknowledgements. 128

Authors

Roxana Bratu is a Research Associate at the School of Slavonic and Eastern European Studies/University College London, UK, (r.bratu@ucl.ac.uk).

Nicholas Charron is Principal Investigator for the survey on Quality of Governance and an Associate Professor at the Quality of Government Institute, University of Gothenburg, Sweden, (nicholas.charron@pol.gu.se).

Valentina Dimulescu is a Policy Researcher at the Romanian Academic Society, Bucharest, Romania, (valentina.dimulescu@sar.org.ro).

Madalina Doroftei is a Project Manager at the Romanian Academic Society, Bucharest, Romania, (madalina.doroftei@gmail.com).

Mihály Fazekas is a PhD Candidate at the University of Cambridge, UK, (mf436@cam.ac.uk).

Aare Kasemets, PhD, is a Researcher at the Estonian Academy of Security Sciences, Tallinn, Estonia and Senior Research Fellow at the European Research Centre for Anti-Corruption and State-Building, Hertie School of Governance, Berlin, Germany, (aare.kasemets@sisekaitse.ee).

Lawrence Peter King, PhD, is a Professor at the University of Cambridge, UK, (lk285@cam.ac.uk).

Roberto Martínez B. Kukutschka is a Junior Researcher at the European Research Centre for Anti-Corruption and State-Building, Hertie School of Governance, Berlin, Germany, (kukutschka@hertie-school.org).

Alina Mungiu-Pippidi, PhD, is a Professor of Democracy Studies at the Hertie School of Governance and Director of the European Research Centre for Anti-Corruption and State-Building, Berlin, Germany, (pippidi@hertie-school.org).

Raluca Pop is a Policy Researcher at the Romanian Academic Society, Bucharest, Romania, (ralucpop@gmail.com).

István János Tóth, PhD, is Co-director at the Corruption Research Centre, Budapest, Hungary, (tothij@econ.core.hu).

All these contributions were given as part of the European Union Seventh Framework Research Project ANTICORRP (Anti-corruption Policies Revisited: Global Trends and European Responses to the Challenge of Corruption).

Executive Summarry

This policy report reviews the lessons learned from the three European political regions researched by the research project ANTICORRP in the first year of the project: the European Union, the South-Eastern Europe and the Former Soviet Union (FSU). Given the large variation across countries, recommendations are different for the three regions, and they are based on the corruption model presented in these regional reports, as well as on the more specific policy data presented in the Romanian, Estonian and Hungarian case studies.

The Anticorruption Report 1 offers five contributions to the objectives of the ANTICORRP project and ten recommendations to European policymakers.

First It contributes to a definition of corruption which includes both 'legal' and 'illegal' aspects by showing public opinion evidence that Europeans see favouritism as corrupt (chapter 8). Chapters 6 and 7 show solid evidence that favouritism of businesses by government, preferential allocation of public funds and more generally favouritism in public services and law enforcement are problems in many European countries and specifically in relation with EU funds.

Second It offers two types of change sensitive corruption indicators which are not perception based (chapters 2, 3, 6, 7 - a review in 9) and which can be used to estimate corruption risk at country and sector level, as well as impact of anticorruption interventions..

Third It offers a policy meaningful classification of corruption risk per country based on the policy determinants of corruption, which is the main basis for recommendations in this report. If we can establish a statistically significant link between a certain policy determinant of corruption and the resulting quality of governance it becomes easier to propose grounded and effective paths of action. The report shows this methodology in chapters 2 and 3, followed then in concluding chapter 9.

Fourth It offers significant statistics on the policy consequences of corruption, as well as the causes, in chapters 2, 6 and 7. Corruption bolsters deficits on behalf of discretionary spending (and hurts investment in public health and education), reduces tax collection, detriments the absorption rate of EU funds, and further generates vulnerable employment and brain drain. This study estimates that if EU member states would all manage to control corruption at the Danish level, tax collection in Europe would bring in yearly about 323 billion more, so the double of current EU budget for 2013. Corruption also affects free market competition.

Fifth It offers a documentation of quality of government at regional level across 24 European countries, based on the largest governance survey in Europe to-date (reported in chapter 8).

The ten generic recommendations, detailed in chapter 9, are:

1. Effective anticorruption policies are broad good governance policies not based solely on repression.

2. There are serious limitations of international approaches to national anticorruption which should be considered at all times.

3. Policies which do not pass a cost-effective examination, either due to very high costs (including political), or proven lack of impact should be discarded.

4. Reducing administrative opportunities for corruption is essential.

5. Reducing fiscal opportunities for corruption plays a very large role and austerity can help anticorruption if it is exercised on behalf of discretionary (government investment) and not universalistic spending (education).

6. The auditing mechanisms of EU funds should be refined and connected to an impact evaluation of funds.

7. Public audit capacity should be increased in unconventional forms, for instance by cooperation with the private and third sector.

8. Judicial autonomy and accountability should be permanently and publicly monitored.

9. National civil society capability for monitoring governance and controlling corruption at both national and local levels should be increased and applied to EU cohesion and assistance funds in particular.

10. An economically depressed media faces high risk of capture and needs support to be able to enforce its role as good governance watchdog.

1. Methodology

Defining corruption is such a controversial business that the United Nations Convention against Corruption (UNCAC, put into force on 14 December 2005) does not even attempt it, stating instead in article 1.c that it will 'promote integrity, accountability and proper management of public affairs and public property'. It also states in articles 7 (public sector) and 9 (procurement), the modern principles of efficiency, transparency, merit, equity and objectivity as the only accepted norms for governance. The European Union signed the United Nations Convention against Corruption (UNCAC) in 2005.

The most frequent definition of individual corruption in current literature is "the abuse of public office for private gain" (Tanzi & Davoodi 1997), with variants such as 'abuse of power' or 'abuse of entrusted authority'. Corruption is nearly always defined as a *deviation from the norm* (Scott 1972) because it presumes that authority or office are entrusted to someone not to promote private gain of any kind (for self or others) but to promote the public interest, in fairness and impartiality. *In the current report we define 'control of corruption' as the capacity of a society to constrain corrupt behaviour in order to enforce the norm of individual integrity in public service and politics and to uphold a state which is free from the capture of particular interests and thus able to promote social welfare.*

One more report on corruption might seem superfluous, as evidence shows that corruption is resilient and does not easily change from year to year. There is, however, a certain novelty to our approach, which is grounded in some of the previous work by the World Bank (Klitgaard 1988; Tanzi & Davoodi 1997; Huther & Shah 2000), but rather different from some of the current anticorruption approaches, for by using theory and inferential statistics we have outlined the causes and consequences of corruption. We have eliminated structural causes which cannot be changed such as the age of a democracy, the former presence of a Communist regime, modernization features and so on, and have developed a powerful explanatory model based only on such factors as can be influenced by human agency. We have then used our statistical model to propose recommendations which can address not only the corruption that is the end result but the whole complex of factors explaining why corruption is not checked by a particular government and society. In other words we point out where control of corruption fails. Control of corruption is a complex equilibrium and the lack of progress during the last fifteen years of anticorruption is due at least in part to the illusion that a few silver bullets can fix it, while its deeper causes are ignored.

Corruption cannot be measured directly due to its elusive and informal nature (a socially undesirable and hidden behaviour) and the difficulty of separating the control of corruption from corruption itself. For instance, if Germany has opened more files on the basis of the OECD anti-bribery convention than other EU countries, does that mean that German businessmen more commonly offer bribes when doing business abroad, or that Germany has actually been more active in enforcing the convention when compared to other countries? The same applies to the number of convictions: notoriously corrupt countries have convicted very few people for corruption, as the judiciary is itself part of the corrupt networks of power and privilege. Due to such limitations therefore, corruption is currently measured in three broad ways:

By gathering the informed views of relevant stakeholders. They include surveys of firms, public officials, experts and citizens. Those data sources can be used separately or in aggregate measures which combine information from many places such as Transparency International's Corruption Perception Index or the World Bank Control of Corruption. Many such sources exist, and they have been aggregated in the two mentioned indexes since 1996. Those are in fact the only available data sources that currently permit large-scale trans-national comparisons and monitoring of corruption over time.

By surveying countries' institutional arrangements, such as procurement practices, budget transparency, and so on. That does not measure actual corruption but rather the risk of corruption occurring. The country coverage is limited to certain developing countries and is not regularly updated. Examples include Global Integrity Index, or the national Integrity Systems of Transparency International.

By audits of specific sectors or projects with the goal of understanding if the allocation of public resources is fair and universal, or particularistic and corrupt. They can be purely financial audits or more specific assessments to measure the efficiency or impartiality of public investment. Such audits can provide information about malfeasance in specific projects but cannot be generalized to more general country-wide corruption, so they are not suited to comparisons between countries nor for monitoring over time (Kaufmann, Kraay & Mastruzzi 2006).

Table 1. Indicators for measuring corruption by data collection type

INDICATORS	Comparison across countries	Comparison across time or before/after intervention	Observations
Perception of corruption, experts, general population, firms	YES	YES, but not fully reliable, as we have proof that other factors matter (for instance, the perceived economic situation)	Highly relevant, but also highly subjective
Experience of corruption experts, general population, firms, government agencies, state units	YES	YES; some limitations apply related to openness in confessing socially undesirable behaviour	Both relevant and objective, with the problem of low response (under-reporting) to overcome

Institutional control of corruption features (permanent and response driven)	YES	Very limited; we have evidence that no correlation exists between institutional equipment for controlling corruption and corruption itself	Highly objective, but frequently irrelevant; those proposed here were all tested for significance in relation with CPI, ICRG or CoC
Audits and investigations	NO	YES, if repeated	Should be organized on specific problems/countries

A good study of corruption in a country should triangulate carefully, by employing all the above methods. We have a few such studies from Europe, mostly for Italy and new member countries from post-communist Europe. The challenge remains of acquiring data to allow comparison between countries, and over time which allows us to record change, and current indexes are not very good at that. Transparency International´s (TI) Corruption Perception Index (CPI) cannot be used to compare over time and the World Bank´s Control of Corruption (CoC) is notoriously insensitive to change. Until suitable indicators are developed, tracing the progress of anticorruption policies by sector or by country over time will remain a challenge. However, discarding the data that is available as being based merely on perception is wrong. Both experience and perception data can be reported and may be compared, and if in separate measurements experts and the general population rate a country similarly it becomes obvious that perceptions are based on similar experience and therefore grounded in reality.

Table 2 shows the correlations between measurements which differ widely in method and time: Control of corruption and CPI, aggregated index scores, a World Economic Forum expert survey score and two general population surveys, TI´s Global Corruption Barometer (GCB) and the Eurobarometer. Those questions asking for an assessment of corruption at national level correlate significantly at over 70% so they are highly consistent across sources. Other questions are more ambiguously phrased which has led to survey error, for example in the Eurobarometer 'major' national problem question which leaves the definition of 'major' up to respondents. However, the relationship between surveys by experts and those by citizens over different years and even with varying vocabulary is, by and large, remarkably consistent and validates corruption indexes and perception indicators – provided always that the questions put are professional, not vague and not leading. Such a validation process is necessary because we plan to use one of those indexes, Control of Corruption, as our main dependent variable in this analytical exercise. Furthermore, due to the scarcity of data down the years our analysis is necessarily limited to a cross sectional analysis of EU member states. In other words, we have 27 observations – as many as the member states. Nevertheless our statistical model was tested on the Hertie School global database of 191 countries and once again the results were remarkably consistent, proving that the data can be safely used for this analysis.

Table 2. Correlations between different corruption indicators

	Perception of corruption public officials	Perception of corruption political parties	% of respondents who agree that corruption is a major problem in the country	% of respondents who agree that there is corruption in national institutions	% of respondents who agree that there is corruption in local institutions	% of respondents who agree that there is corruption in regional institutions	WGI Control of Corruption estimate (2010)	Quality of government	Corruption Perception Index (TI)	Diversion of public funds, 1-7 (best)	N	Source
Perception of corruption public officials	1										21	Global Corruption Barometer (2010)
Perception of corruption political parties	,731**	1									21	Global Corruption Barometer (2010)
% of respondents who agree that corruption is a major problem in the country	-,730**	-,829**	1								27	Eurobarometer 374 (2011)
% of respondents who agree that there is corruption in national institutions	,749**	,847**	-,948**	1							27	Eurobarometer 374 (2011)
% of respondents who agree that there is corruption in local institutions	,756**	,855**	-,949**	,982**	1						27	Eurobarometer 374 (2011)
% of respondents who agree that there is corruption in regional institutions	,748**	,857**	-,907**	,970**	,961**	1					27	Eurobarometer 374 (2011)
WGI Control of Corruption estimate (2010)	-,722**	-,707**	,782**	-,784**	-,816**	-,778**	1				27	Worldwide Governance Indicators (2010)
Quality of government	-,677**	-,626**	,706**	-,691**	-,737**	-,687**	,951**	1			27	ICRG (2010)
Perception of corruption (TI)	-,722**	-,699**	,780**	-,777**	-,810**	-,765**	,991**	,931**	1		27	Corruption Perception Index (2010)
Diversion of public funds, 1-7 (best)	-,706**	-,690**	,749**	-,766**	-,788**	-,776**	,960**	,913**	,962**	1	27	Global Competitiveness Report (2010-11)

** Correlation is significant at the 0.01 level (2-tailed)

This first Anticorruption Report covers the European continent. We divided it for study in three areas: European Union member states South-Eastern Europe and former Soviet Union. This division is justified by the different legal and political regimes operating in these three areas. From an EU perspective, an EU anticorruption policy exists in nearly all this territory, either under the anticorruption mechanism of the European Commission (EU member states, managed by DG Home), or enlargement or EU neighbourhood policy (Russia is an exception). The report will present comparative data on all three regions, followed by a succession of three case studies in relation to the European Union: a problem country for both corruption and EU funds (Romania), an average country which surveys and our field research show to be more problematic than previously believed (Hungary) and a champion of anticorruption, the global 'achiever' of good governance, Estonia.

References

Kaufmann, Daniel; Kraay, Aart & Mastruzzi, Massimo 2006: "Measuring Corruption: Myths and Realities", World Bank, Washington, DC

Klitgaard, Robert 1988: *Controlling Corruption*, Berkley CA: University of California Press

Huther, Jeff, & Shah, Anwar 2000: "Anticorruption Policies and Programs: A Framework for Evaluation", *Policy Research Working Paper* 2501, World Bank, Washington, DC

Tanzi, Vito & Davoodi, Hamid R. 1997: "Corruption, Public Investment, and Growth", *IMF Working Paper* 97/139

Scott, James C. 1972: *Political Corruption*, Englewood Cliffs, N.J., Prentice-Hall

The List of Data Sources

- Bertelsmann Stiftung, Bertelsmann Sustainable Governance Indicators - <www.sgi-network.org/>
- European Commission, "Digitizing Public Services in Europe: Putting ambition into action-9th Benchmark Measurement" - <ec.europa.eu/information_society/newsroom/cf/itemdetail.cfm?item_id=6537>
- Eurostat - <www.ec.europa.eu/eurostat>
- Freedom House, "Freedom in the World" - <http://www.freedomhouse.org/report-types/freedom-world>
- Hertie School of Governance, "Contextual Choices in Fighting Corruption: Lessons Learned" - <www.hertie-school.org/facultyandresearch/projects/research-projects/transitions-to-good-governance-contextual-choices-in-fighting-corruption>
- International Labour Organization, Laborsta database - <laborsta.ilo.org/default.html>
- Inter-Parliamentary Union, "Women in national Parliament data" - <www.ipu.org/wmn-e/classif-arc.htm>
- Quality of Government Institute, QoG standard database and QoG basic database - <www.qog.pol.gu.se/data/datadownloads>
- Romanian Academic Society - <www.sar.org.ro>
- Special Eurobarometer Survey 374, "Corruption" - <ec.europa.eu/public_opinion/archives/ebs/ebs_374_en.pdf>
- Standard Eurobarometer 72, - <http://ec.europa.eu/public_opinion/archives/eb/eb72/eb72_en.htm>
- Transparency International, "Corruption Perception Index 2010" and "Global corruption Barometer 2010" - <www.transparency.org>
- World Bank database - <data.worldbank.org>
- World Economic Forum, "Global Competitiveness Report 2010-2011" - <www3.weforum.org/docs/WEF_GlobalCompetitivenessReport_2010-11.pdf>
- Worldwide Governance Indicators - <www.govindicators.org>

2. European Union Member States

ALINA MUNGIU-PIPPIDI
AND ROBERTO MARTÍNEZ B. KUKUTSCHKA

For many years corruption was seen as a problem only of developing countries, while the European Union (EU) on the contrary was the temple of the rule of law, exporting good governance both to its own peripheries and worldwide. Many European countries indeed remain among the best governed in the world, although the downfall of the Santer Commission on charges of corruption, the enlargement of the EU by its incorporation of new member countries with unfinished transitions, and the economic crisis all strongly indicate that control of corruption is difficult to build and hard to sustain. Older member countries Greece, Italy, Portugal and Spain have all regressed (See **Figure 1**) rather than progressed since they joined – the first two of them to worrying levels – and that has raised doubts about the EU's transformative effect on its members.

Data published by the World Bank and taken from the Worldwide Governance Indicator (WGI) Control of Corruption offer a global picture which is no less challenging. Of 196 countries only 21 (mostly Caribbean and Balkan) showed statistically significant improvement since 1996, and 27 countries significantly regressed leaving only fewer than a quarter of countries around the world with a reasonable control over corruption. Although on average more than 90% of Europeans in the 27 EU member countries declare that they were not asked for a bribe last year, 79% fully or partially agree that corruption exists in their national institutions, although with insignificant differences between regional or local levels of government. **Almost half of all Europeans (47%) think that the level of corruption in their country has risen over the past three years, with national politicians (57%), and officials responsible for awarding public tenders (47%) the most likely to be blamed for such behaviour.**[1] In new East European member countries, with the exception of Estonia and Slovenia, more than 10% had directly encountered some form of bribery during the previous year. The gap between the widespread perception of corruption and limited experience of actual bribery shows that Europeans consider other types of behaviour as well as bribery to be corrupt, for instance the peddling of political influence, favouritism or clientelism.

---

[1] Special Eurobarometer Survey 374, "Corruption", available at <http://ec.europa.eu/public_opinion/archives/ebs/ebs_374_en.pdf>

Figure 1. Progress and regress in the European Union – selected countries

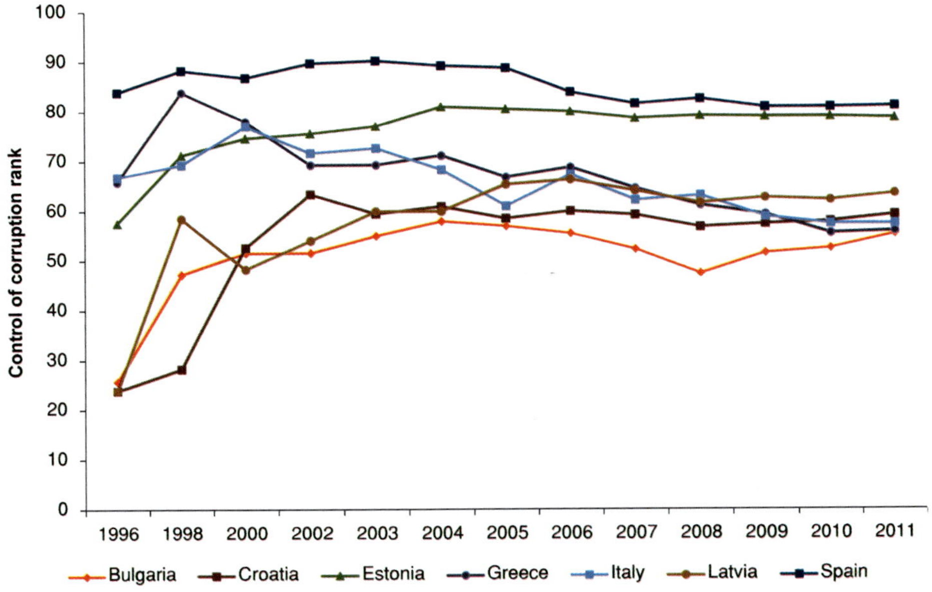

Data source: Worldwide Governance Indicators (1996-2011)

I. Consequences of corruption in EU

Our ability to measure corruption enables us to gather evidence of its detrimental consequences, unlike the literature previous to these measurements, which highlighted the positive functions of corruption: as an effective way to compensate for functional deficiencies in the official structure (Merton 1957: 73), an alternative to revolution and civil war (Bayley 1966; Dwivedi 1967; Huntington 1968); as a means to achieve political stability (Huntington 1968) and to integrate elite and non-elite members (Nye 1967); the oil for the wheels of the economy (Huntington 1968: 68); and as a lubricant for the economic development of modernizing countries (Leys 1965; Bayley 1966; Nye 1967). The possibility of measuring corruption and thus the ability to relate it to other indicators has reversed those arguments. For instance, the currently most-quoted corruption paper, presently available from oxfordjournals.org, is "Corruption and growth" by the economist Paulo Mauro of the International Monetary Fund. The association between corruption and growth raised the interest of social science, media and policymakers to its current heights, although findings remain disputed.

Using a method similar to Mauro's but with a different dependent variable, this report examines the impact of corruption on a number of areas essential to Europeans. Seeing the complexity of economic crises, we have not directly measured the impact of corruption on growth. Control of corruption is certainly strongly associated with high levels of development, and we use development as a control to test the relationship between corruption and a number of negative outcomes, as we will argue that a significant proportion of corruption affects social welfare in a variety of ways.

1. The impact of corruption on public investment

A long-standing controversy exists over whether big government is the source of corruption or the solution to it. In Europe, big government, when measured as the proportion of total spending from GDP, is associated with less corruption, not more; while the opposite is true for Latin America. It seems rather obvious when you consider that the Scandinavian countries, as the least corrupt countries in Europe, are big spenders traditionally associated with social welfare (Rothstein & Uslaner 2005). But what if, under certain conditions, *the type of spending rather than its size* is more prone to feed corruption? We suggest that the opportunity for discretionary spending in the absence of adequate constraints is what fuels grand corruption rather than the actual amount of spending. For instance, corrupt politicians tend to orient public spending so as to maximize income for their clients and political sponsors, which generally means that the money is channelled to projects resulting in large government contracts which are attributed to favoured contractors. The problem with that – even presuming that no extra costs would be incurred by the government and that such projects do add something to social welfare - is that such client-directed spending tends to be unaffordable and so squeezes investment in other areas. If we are right, then we should find that the more corrupt EU states are associated with greater project spending (see **Figure 2**), and less social investment, for instance in health programmes (see **Figure 3**). *The most corrupt European countries indeed spend significantly less on health.* They are also those where citizens complain more loudly of corruption in their healthcare system.

Figure 2. Corruption and projects spending[2]

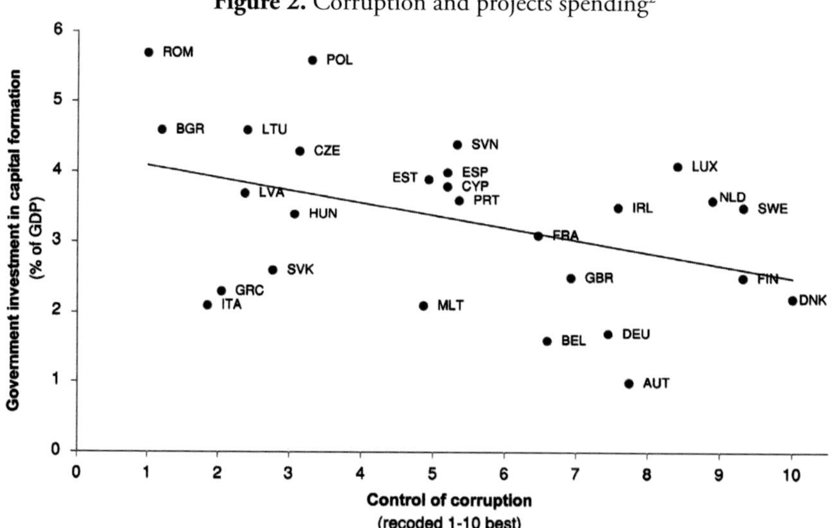

Data source: World Bank Database, Gross capital formation (% of GDP)

---

[2] Gross capital formation (% of GDP); General government gross fixed capital formation (ESA95 code P.51) consists of resident producers' acquisitions, less disposals of fixed assets during a given period plus certain additions to the value of non-produced assets realized by the productive activity of government producer or units. Fixed assets are tangible or intangible assets produced as outputs from processes of production that are themselves used repeatedly, or continuously, in processes of production for more than one year, available at <http://data.worldbank.org/indicator/NE.GDI.TOTL.ZS>

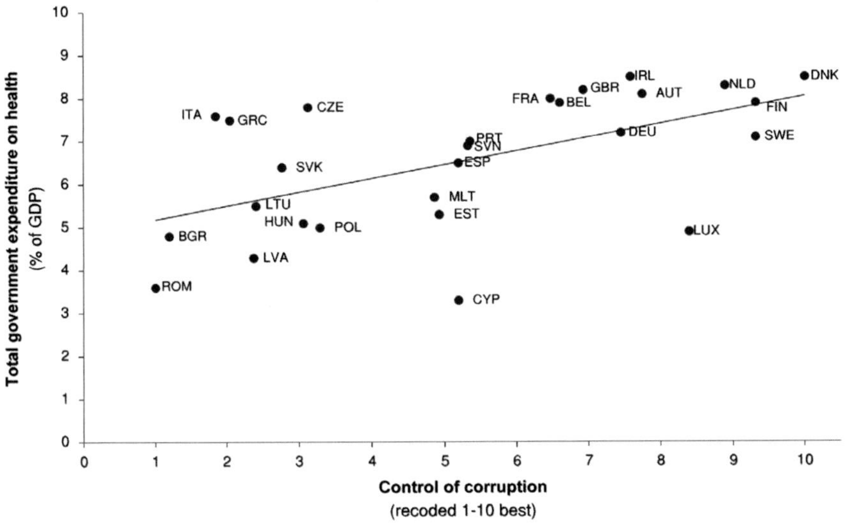

Data source: Eurostat, "General government expenditure by function (COFOG)"

Romania and Bulgaria are at one extreme, spending little on health and far more on projects, with Denmark at the opposite extreme. Of course, part of the explanation is development: Romania and Bulgaria are far less developed than Denmark so they still require construction of a modern transport infrastructure and so on. However, the underfunding of healthcare creates systemic corruption problems only within the health system. For example, the state in Bulgaria, Romania or Lithuania claims to provide medical treatment at prices in line with the capability of the state health insurance system, but the reality is that the insurance system is doubly inadequate. First and foremost because if their claims were true and everyone in need began to request the available services like screening or surgery, state insurance funds would be insufficient to cover even a quarter of the resulting costs. Second, because the state pretends to believe that doctors and nurses can do their work for the wages they are paid, which is simply not possible in those new EU member countries from the East. The salaries of doctors and nurses in Romania and Bulgaria for example are on average below 500 USD per month. The shortfall between the official cost of services and the real cost of the work is therefore offset by 'gifts' paid by patients to supplement their insurance cover and that is how a balance is established between supply and demand and how more realistic prices are set. Can such goings-on be considered perhaps a clever way for governments to supplement the income of the heath sector without introducing an unpopular tax, with the benefit resulting from investment in projects offering some form of compensation? Not really, as returns from public investment are also the lowest in the most corrupt countries, while health systems are chronically underfinanced.

Now; if we look at Greece or more particularly Italy, those two countries are the outliers of the corruption-related association outlined, especially where health spending is

---

[3] Health spending is measured as total general government expenditure on health as share of GDP, available at <http://appsso.eurostat.ec.europa.eu/nui/show.do?dataset=gov_a_exp&lang=en>

concerned. Being richer than Bulgaria, Romania and Lithuania, Greece and Italy have managed to spend on health as well as on projects, but as one would expect that is a recipe for fiscal deficit.

2. The impact of corruption on fiscal deficit

The mechanism described in the previous section, of client-directed spending concentrated on a few beneficiaries over and above social spending spread evenly among everyone entitled to it, makes for a very costly combination. Using the most recent data we discover that a significant association does indeed exist between corruption and budget balance at an EU level (see **Figure 4**; see also Kaufmann 2010). There a few outliers to what is otherwise a clear association between low corruption and a budget balance very close to zero as seen in Denmark and Finland, and high corruption and a poor balance as in Greece, Romania or Latvia. The result robust with development controls, and shows that there is an undeniable link between corruption and overspending.

Figure 4. Corruption and balance of Government budget[4]

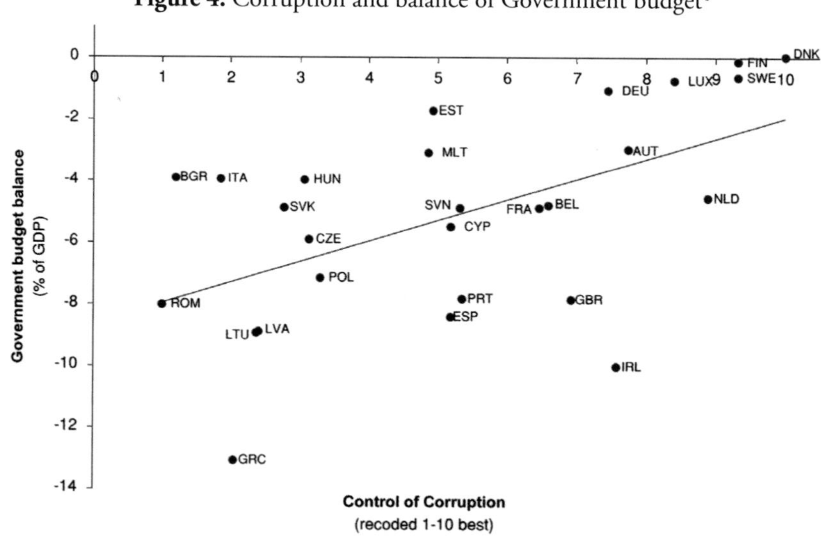

Data source: World Economic Forum, "Global Competitiveness Report 2010-2011"

3. The impact of corruption on tax collection

A deficit is not created by spending alone, and corruption in all countries lying below the rank of 65 in the Control of Corruption WBI rankings tends to cut across sectors. Therefore the hope that perhaps a country which overspends due to corruption might compensate for that in other areas, by collecting its income efficiently, is plainly wrong. At the level of EU-27 the more corrupt states are those with the worse performance on tax collection too (see **Figure 5**). The association is significant and robust, with Lithuania, Romania Bulgaria in the worst positions and Denmark again in the lead. Italy and Ireland

---

[4] Fiscal deficit/surplus; Government gross budget balance as a percentage of GDP, available at <http://www3. weforum.org/docs/WEF_GlobalCompetitivenessReport_2010-11.pdf>

are outliers, Italy showing collection better than its poor corruption rating would predict, and Ireland with collection efficiency inferior to its good score for its control of corruption.

A simple estimate on the basis of regression analysis shows that if EU member states would all manage to control corruption at the Danish level, tax collection in Europe would bring in yearly about 323 billion more, so the double of current EU budget for 2013.

Figure 5. Corruption and tax collection[5]

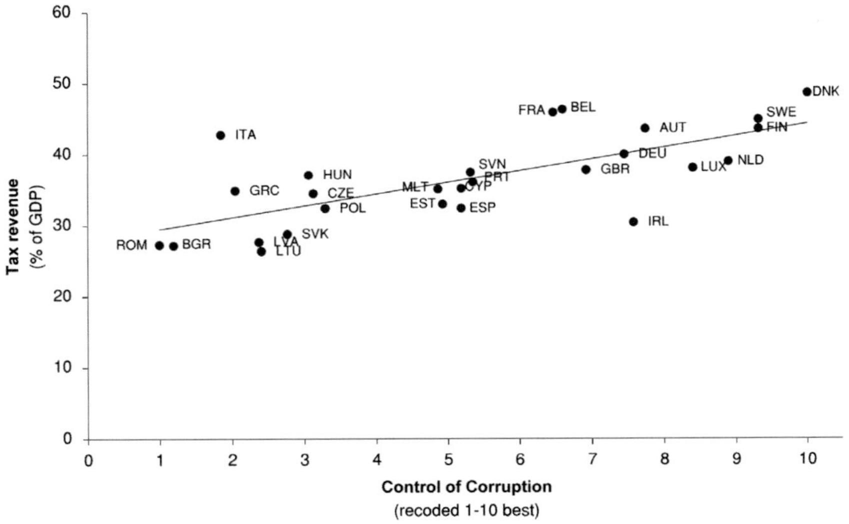

Data source: Eurostat, "Tax revenue statistics"

4. The impact of corruption on vulnerable employment

The link between corruption and the informal economy is complex in developing countries (Dreher & Schneider 2010). For the European Union, the problem is somewhat different. Being the most economically developed polity in the world, we expect the EU to be able to control its informal sector and to protect its employees. But does it? Regressing corruption on vulnerable employment we again find significant association, robust even when a control for development is added to the model. Corruption leads to a significant increase in the number of vulnerable employees (see **Figure 6**), which in its turn influences tax collection and an array of other factors. Romania seems an outlier, as it has even more vulnerable employment than its level of corruption would predict because it is the most rural country in Europe with more than 30% engaged in subsistence farming. However, the model fits Italy very well as too nearly all other countries and with Denmark again the perfect fit and the best performer, with Romania in worst position.

---

[5] Tax revenue to GDP ratio. Total receipts from taxes and social contributions (including imputed social contributions) as percentage of GDP, available at <http://epp.eurostat.ec.europa.eu/statistics_explained/index.php/Tax_revenue_statistics>

Figure 6. Corruption and vulnerable employment[6]

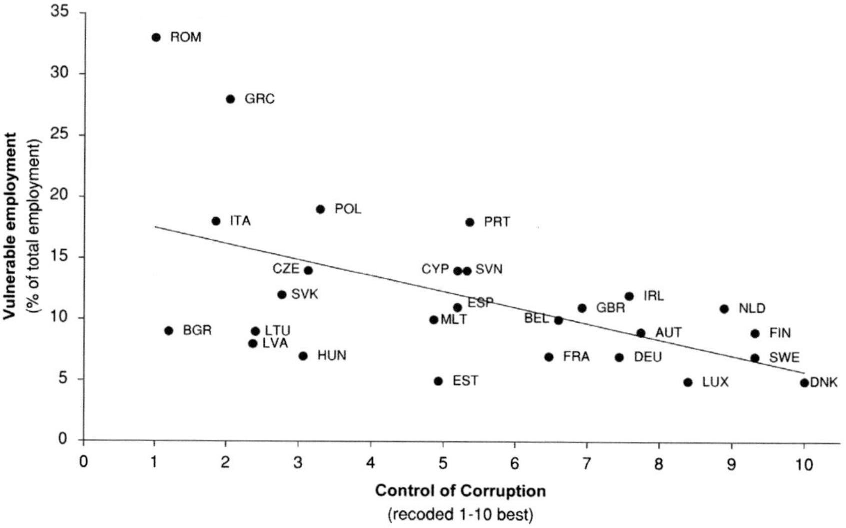

Data source: World Bank database, "Vulnerable employment"

5. The impact of corruption on gender equality

Denmark and Romania are again the perfect opposites when it comes to the impact of corruption on gender equality (see **Figure 7**). The significant association between the two variables has long been known, although it has received quite different interpretations (Sung 2003). It is also strong at the EU level, especially when the indicators measuring women in politics are considered (the association with gender pay gap is not significant). In other words, more corrupt countries do not pay women significantly less, but do significantly restrict their access to positions of power. We interpret that finding here on the side of those who argue that this is not about women, but about governance. Where power and privilege are concentrated in certain networks and groups which manage to control access to public jobs, where in other words societies are dominated by favouritism and corruption, we find that weaker groups - as a rule women and minorities - tend to be excluded. **The presence of few women in Parliament is a significant indicator of the presence of favouritism in political life.**

[6] Vulnerable employment means unpaid family workers and own-account workers as a percentage of total employment, available at <http://data.worldbank.org/indicator/SL.EMP.VULN.ZS>

Figure 7. Women in parliament and corruption[7]

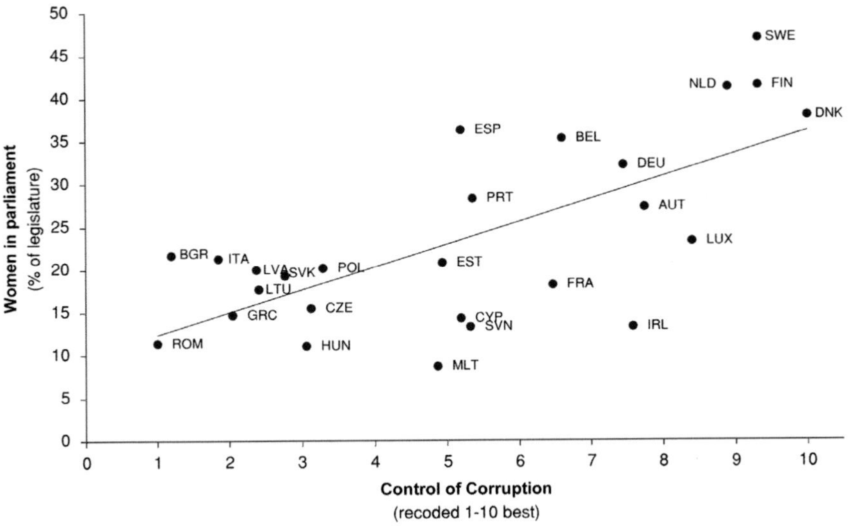

Data source: Inter-Parliamentary Union Homepage, "Women in National Parliaments"

6. The impact of corruption on the "brain-drain"

Corruption significantly increases the brain-drain. Corrupt societies which channel access through patronage and corruption therefore discourage meritocracy and encourage talented people to seek recognition elsewhere. The association is highly significant, controlling for development at the level of the EU-27. That is particularly revealing considering that the EU is a common labour market. Apart from language barriers there are few obstacles to internal migration in the European Union, and seeing that some new member countries from Eastern Europe have a highly educated population but high levels of favouritism and corruption, the brain-drain is a major threat to their economic recovery. The risk is faced not only by Romania, Lithuania, Latvia and Bulgaria, but by Italy and Greece too (See **Figure 8**).

---

[7] This indicator refers to the composition of the parliament at the end of the corresponding year (1990-2009). In bicameral systems data is taken for the lower house. It is used as a proxy for how much women are represented and how much their role in society is recognized, available at <http://www.ipu.org/wmn-e/classif-arc. htm>

Figure 8. The "Brain-drain" and the control of corruption[8]

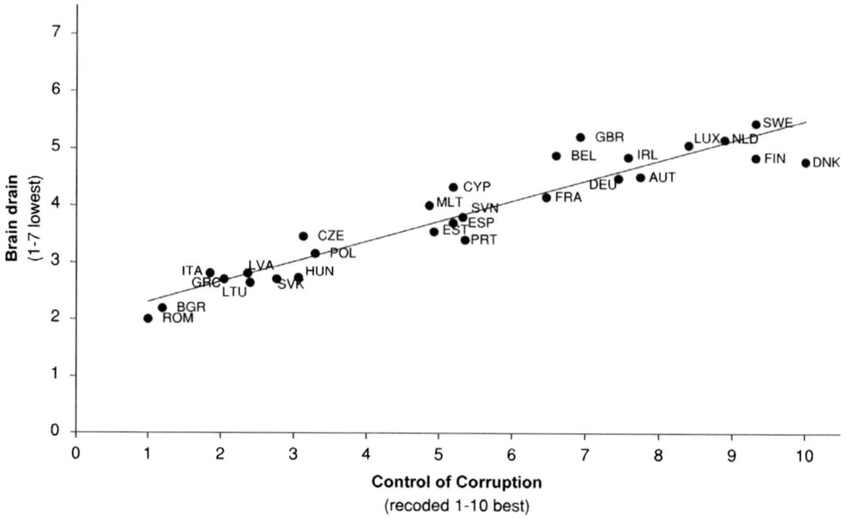

Data source: World Economic Forum, "Global Competitiveness Report 2010-2011"

7. The impact of corruption on the absorption of EU funds

Finally, the existence of corruption is a significant barrier to the effective absorption of EU Cohesion Funds, even ignoring the effectiveness with which such funds reach their development objectives. It simply means that the more corrupt a country is, the less funding it succeeds in attracting for it to spend and be reimbursed by the EU from Cohesion Funds (See **Figure 9**). That leads to a vicious circle, as such funds are intended to foster development, in the absence of which corruption thrives. Corruption is obviously not the only factor affecting absorption: Lithuania and Poland are less corrupt than Romania, Bulgaria and Italy, but the difference cannot fully explain the wide differences in their performance in the absorption of EU funds.

---

[8] Weighted average of the answers to the question "Does your country retain and attract talented people?". Answers range from 1 (the best and brightest normally leave to pursue opportunities in other countries) to 7 (there are many opportunities for talented people within the country, available at <http://www3.weforum.org/docs/ WEF_GlobalCompetitivenessReport_2010-11.pdf>

Figure 9. Absorption rate and corruption[9]

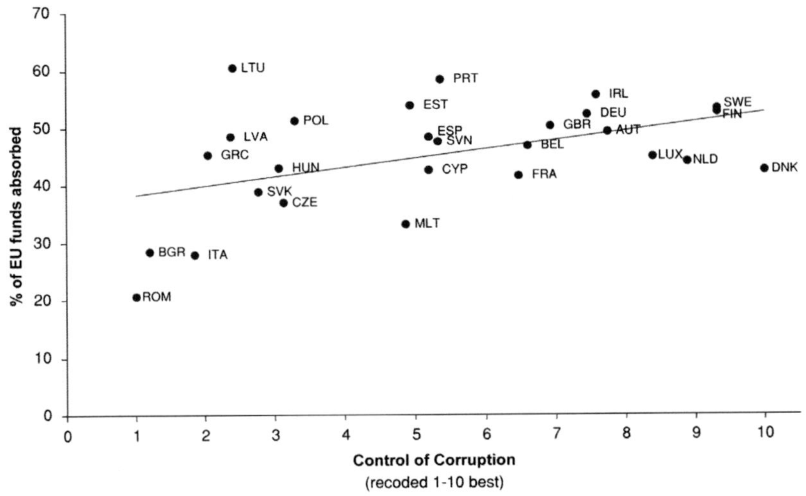

Data source: European Commission, "EU cohesion funding- key statistics"

II. Leaders and laggards

The EU likes to think of itself as enjoying the best rule of law and control of corruption in the world. International corruption rankings annually give many EU countries high marks for their capacity to control corruption, with ten countries regularly in the upper quarter of the best-governed countries in the world. Over the years, the hope that the EU's liberalized and harmonized markets and strong rule of law would determine the convergence of Italy, Greece, and the newer member states from the East has somewhat faded. Excepting Estonia and Slovenia, both of which quickly rose to join the leading group, hopes for the others did not materialize. Italy and Greece stagnated, even declined. So too did Spain, Portugal and Cyprus, while even Austria and the United Kingdom which were always near the top have recently slipped back somewhat. It is clear that national boundaries remain the boundaries of governance despite the trans-territoriality of crime and, increasingly, the law. Control of corruption is built up within domestic borders: if control fails nationally there is little that international law and conventions can do.

While the research project ANTICORRP will return with a full evaluation of national and sub-national favouritism and corruption next year, for the purpose of the current report we shall highlight only those features which illustrate the dangers of corruption to the common market in certain EU countries. For instance, to what extent is market competition hindered by government favouritism, state capture by corporate interests and corruption? The whole rationale behind the existence of the EU is that a common market will increase economic competitiveness and performance. If certain governments

---

[9] Percentage of the total funds allocated per Member State that has been paid by the Commission, on the basis of claims submitted. It indicates the payment rate for territorial cooperation. These are the combined figures for the European Regional Development Fund, the Cohesion Fund and the European Social Fund, available at <http://ec.europa.eu/regional_policy/thefunds/funding/index_en.cfm>

favour certain companies over others (whether due to political ties, contributions to party finance, bribery, the "pork barrel") the common market is endangered. Authors like Carolyn Warner have previously argued that increased competition due to the common market did not manage to restrain corruption: in fact quite the contrary (Warner 2007).

There is considerable variation among European countries where government favouritism is concerned (see **Figure 10**). The European average is below 4 with the maximum positive score being 7, and only seven countries are significantly above average: the four Scandinavian countries, Germany, the UK and Luxembourg. One new member country, Estonia, has managed to increase its performance to reach the average, while Greece and Italy are level with Romania, Slovakia, the Czech Republic, Latvia, Hungary and Bulgaria, which score the worst. **In other words, in a considerable number of EU member states (MS) we find that even on the core EU matter of the common market, government favouritism is the rule rather than the exception in more than half the countries of the EU (17), when the benchmark should be no fewer than 4 out of 7.**

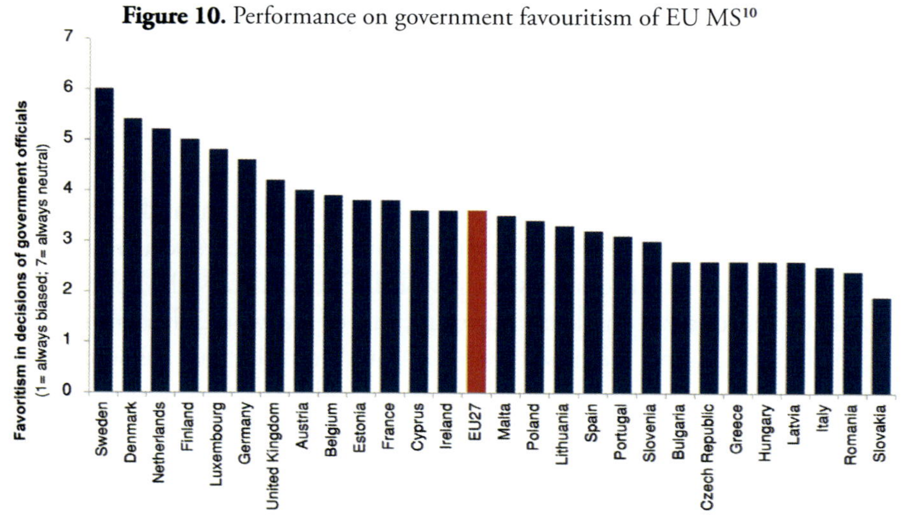

Figure 10. Performance on government favouritism of EU MS[10]

Data source: World Economic Forum, "Global Competitiveness Report 2010-2011"

The second important question is the extent to which the allocation of public funds, including European funds, is affected by discretion due to favouritism, fraud and corruption? (see **Figure 11**). The allocation of public resources should be universal, fair and lawful and not determined by favouritism due to a particular authority or office holder's ties to any company, individual or group. As a Swedish textbook for civil servants specifies: "When implementing laws and policies, government officials shall not take anything about the citizen/case into consideration that is not beforehand stipulated in the policy or the law" (Strömberg 2000).

---

[10] Weighted average of the responses to the question: to what extent do government officials in your country show favouritism to well-connected firms and individuals when deciding upon policies and contracts? Answers range from 1 (always show favouritism) to 7 (never show favouritism), available at <http://www3.weforum.org/docs/ WEF_GlobalCompetitivenessReport_2010-11.pdf>

Data source: World Economic Forum, "Global Competitiveness Report 2010-2011"

While most corruption surveys focus on bribes, once we accept that some EU governments provide market favours for companies in Europe we should question government impartiality in the realm of spending as well, especially since we presented evidence in the previous section that corruption greatly influences the distribution of public spending, channelling more funds into projects as opposed to into universal allocations. Unfortunately there are almost no audits to check on the relevant kind of data and practically no research, with money regularly being poured into new waves of surveys on corruption perception instead of into monitoring of public spending.

What should such monitoring audits look for? First, funds that are distributed only discretionarily, in other words without the transparent logic that would make any other civil servant authorize spending in exactly the same pattern as the particular individual supervising any given transaction which we might care to examine. Second, that the recipients of privileged allocations (transfers, subsidies, public contracts), have some particular tie to the party granting the allocation, a tie which would of course explain why the advantage was granted to them instead of to others. Such ties which could explain favouritism might be political (for instance, more EU funds can be granted to regions where leadership is of the same political persuasion as that of the controllers of funds; or extra-budgetary funds (such as reserve funds of prime ministers as in Slovakia, or of the government, as in Romania) might be distributed to reward political supporters' constituencies against opposition in the national Parliament; or discretionary allocation might be made either on the basis of regional, ethnic or family solidarity; or there might be personal rewards for those who decide allocations (bribes, kickbacks). The UNCAC, as well as the legislation of many countries considers not

---

[11] Weighted average of the answers to the questions: how common is diversion of public funds to companies, individuals, or groups due to corruption? [1 = very common; 7 = never occurs], available at <http://www3.weforum.org/docs/WEF_GlobalCompetitivenessReport_2010-11.pdf>

just bribes but any allocation of that kind as corrupt, but unless we understand how allocations work in general it is difficult to discern if bribes are a way of paying for privilege, or its opposite – a way of buying equal access.

A more eloquent example as an illustration is the fate of international (mostly European) construction companies in the new member country of Romania, where government favouritism is entrenched. The same example could be taken from all countries with similar levels of government favouritism and across all sectors where government contracts are important, and not only infrastructure. What the figure below shows (see **Figure 12**) is turnover and profit of international companies compared to Romanian ones before and after EU accession (2004-2007). Romania's domestic companies thrived after accession when theoretically competition should have increased, with some of the companies making profits of 30% or more during recession years when the entire construction sector contracted nationally, while international ones diminished to near extinction. All the fabulous profits can be explained by government contracts commissioned by Romania's National Companies for Roads, a state operator.

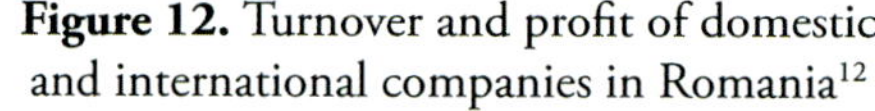

Figure 12. Turnover and profit of domestic and international companies in Romania[12]

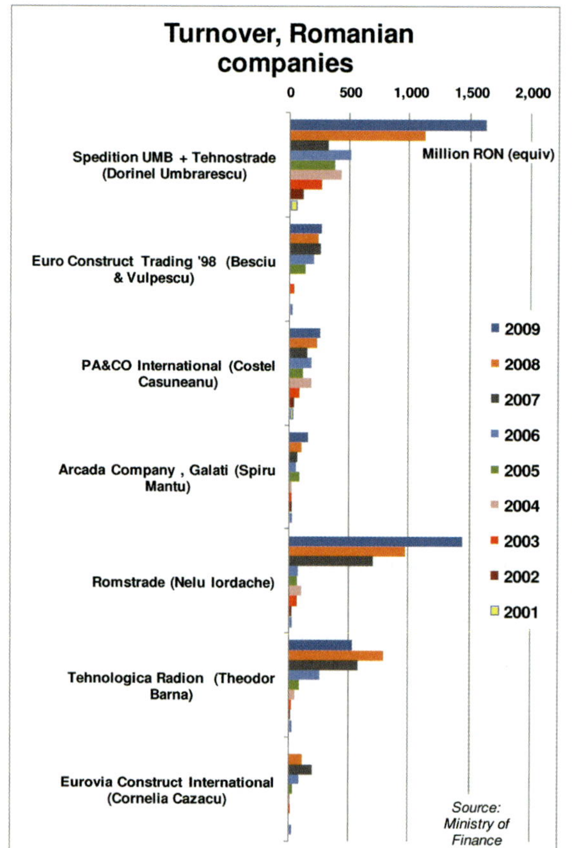

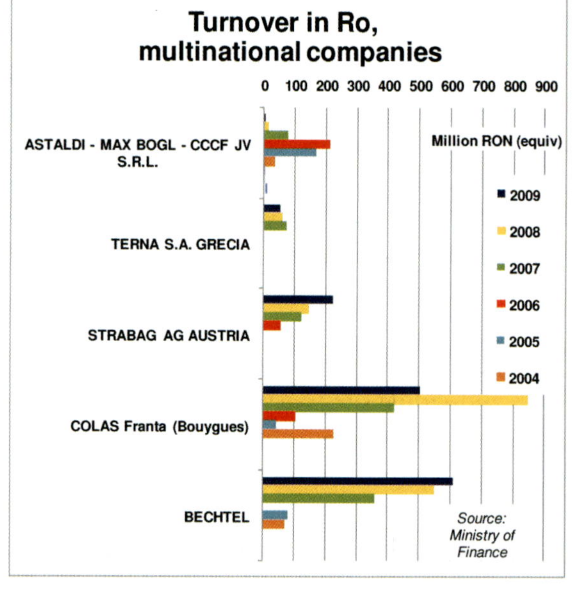

---

[12] Alina Mungiu-Pippidi et al. 2011. Beyond Perception: Has Romania's Governance Improve since 2006? Bucharest: Romanian Academic Society, accessible on <www.sar.org.ro>

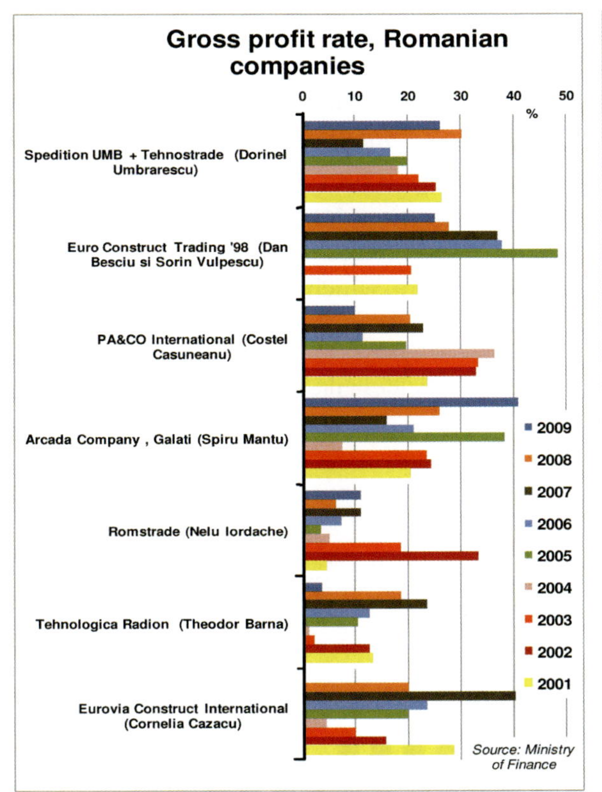

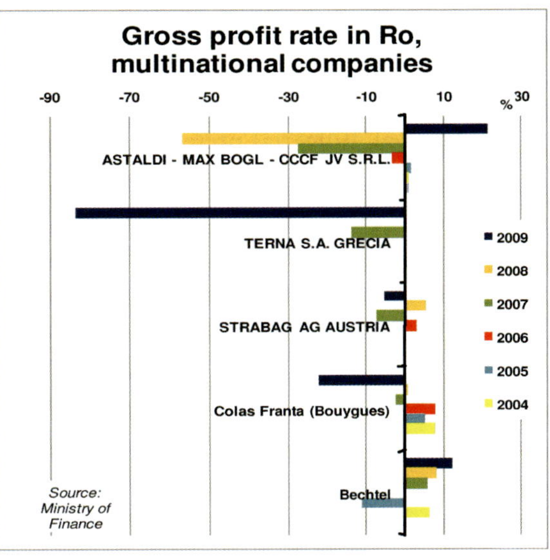

Romanian Academic Society: Annual Policy & Forecast Report, Romania in 2011, p. 14

Why did that not happen before 2007, since appointments to management of the company had always been political? The reason was the pending uncertainty related to Romania's Accession date, whether it would be 2007 or 2008, which made the government reluctant to discriminate so much against European companies prior to Accession. Since the publication of the figures in 2011 one of the most successful domestic entrepreneurs, Nelu Iordache from Romstrade, has been investigated by the OLAF and finally charged by Romanian prosecutors. He had allegedly built a private empire with public funds: the last acquisition - which precipitated his arrest - was the purchase of an aircraft for his company Blueair with the co-financing funds that the Romanian government had advanced for Arad-border highway, an EU-sponsored project which had been stalled for years. Had not Mr. Iordache openly misused that public money, no prosecutors would have considered data presented in **Figure 12** worth investigating, although it clearly shows a non-random distribution and clear discrimination against companies lacking national political connections. Connecting that to the legendary inefficiency of Romania's infrastructure development, we have a complete picture of how corruption can sabotage development intended to be sponsored by EU funds.

Having established how government favouritism is tied in with discretionary allocation of public funds we can go on to ask if ordinary citizens are affected by all this, or does the bulk remain in the area of grand corruption, fiscal deficit and so on? The answer is that citizens are affected, and proportionally so- there is again a correlation between countries with high government favouritism, diversion of public funds and complaints by citizens about poor services.

In a 2012 Eurobarometer the same group of countries (plus Cyprus, Lithuania, Portugal, Bulgaria) present the largest number of citizens complaining that corruption affects them most (see **Figure 13**). The European average is over 30 per cent, which is already problematic – it means after all that a third of citizens complain that they are personally affected by corruption - but in Romania and Greece the figure is above 70 per cent, indicating that we are dealing with policy failure, which cannot be solved by legal means only.

Figure 13. The perception of corruption in daily life in the EU MS[13]

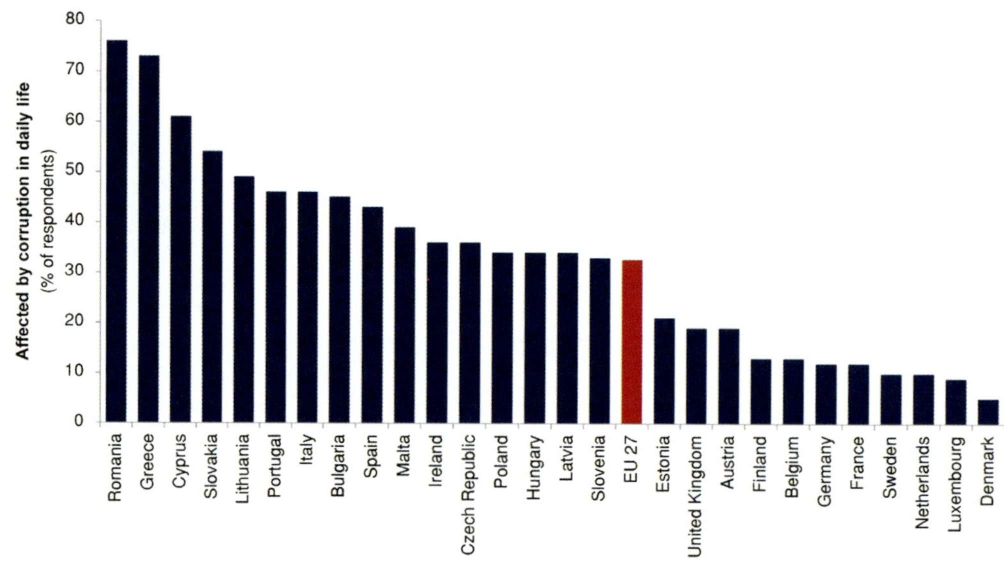

Data source: Special Eurobarometer 374, "Corruption"

The conclusion to be drawn from this very brief review is that for a significant number of MS (i.e. more than half), corruption affects both top government spending decisions and the lives of ordinary people. The proportion is such that a policy approach is needed: with more than half of citizens affected we are no longer discussing corruption as 'deviation', but rather as the norm.

III. Causes of corruption

Leaving aside the moralist literature on corruption, many economists consider that when costs are low and resources and opportunities high, it is rational for an individual to be corrupt. The World Bank's Robert Klitgaard (1988: 75) defined corruption as equilibrium, considering that when monopoly of power and administrative discretion are not checked by accountability, then the result is corruption. The literature on the

---

[13] Percentage of respondents who "totally agree" or "tend to agree" that they are personally affected by corruption in their daily life, available at
<http://ec.europa.eu/public_opinion/archives/ebs/ebs_374_en.pdf>

enforcement of the rule of law (Becker and Stigler 1974), developed in Van Rijckeghem and Weder (1997) also looks for a balance when suggesting that very low wages combined with an absence of corruption detection leads to low control of corruption. Most literature on the national causes of corruption classifies factors as economic, political and cultural or groups the causes into two broad categories: structural factors (population, legacies, religion, past regime) and current government policies pertaining to the control of corruption (economic, but also specific anticorruption policies). We suggest that an explanatory model of corruption at national level is best described as an equilibrium between opportunities (resources) for corruption and deterrents (constraints) imposed by the state and society, as follows:

> Corruption/Control of Corruption = Opportunities (Power Discretion + Material Resources) – Deterrents (Legal + Normative)

Opportunities or resources can be detailed as:

- Discretionary power opportunities due not only to monopoly but also to privileged access under power arrangements other than monopoly or oligopoly – for example, negative social capital networks, cartels and other collusive arrangements, purposely poor regulation encouraging administrative discretion, lack of transparency turning information into privileged capital for power-holders and their relations, and so on.
- Material resources - including state assets, concessions and discretionary budget spending, foreign aid, natural resources in state property, public sector employment, and any other resources which can be used and abused, turned into spoils or generate rents.

Deterrents or constraints can be detailed as:

- Legal: This supposes an autonomous, accountable and effective judiciary able to enforce legislation, as well as a body of effective and comprehensive laws covering conflict of interest and enforcing a clear public-private separation.
- Normative: This implies that existing societal norms endorse public integrity and government impartiality, and permanently and effectively monitor deviations from that norm through public opinion, media, civil society, and a critical electorate.

We have tested this equilibrium formula empirically on a large number of countries to great effect in another paper (Mungiu-Pippidi et al. 2011). Here in this section we shall confine ourselves to reviewing the main significant determinants which cause corruption, with a number of observations applying only to the EU-27. Appendices 1-7 present all during our research several statistical models were tested, but for this report we will focus only on the main determinants of corruption, since no successful anticorruption policy can be enacted without adressing them. We also present sundry solutions from the current anticorruption arsenal which although usually recommended never seem to work. The statistical tests we used (regressions) essentially use a comparative method allowing us to evaluate whether countries which perform better are more or less associated with a certain determinant. When we say that something 'works' or 'does not work' we mean that we find a significant difference in controlling corruption between countries which have adopted that particular practice and those which have not.

We controlled for development in order to 'equalize' countries and to be sure we were not measuring some indirect effect of differences in development across the EU. The proxy we used for development was the human development index, an aggregated index formed from education, life expectancy and income which was devised by the United Nations Development Program.

The following has high impact and influences corruption greatly at the level of the EU-27:

1. **Administrative discretion or "Red tape".** There is a very strong association between red tape and corruption, as excessive regulation is the main instrument used to increase administrative discretion and through it corruption. Greece and Italy are the outstanding cases, as **Figure 14** shows. This indicator is an objective assessment and not subjective, so examining its components leads directly to the problem areas. The same relationship we can see when we look at the association between trade barriers and corruption (see **Figure 15**).

Figure 14. Ease of doing business and corruption[14]

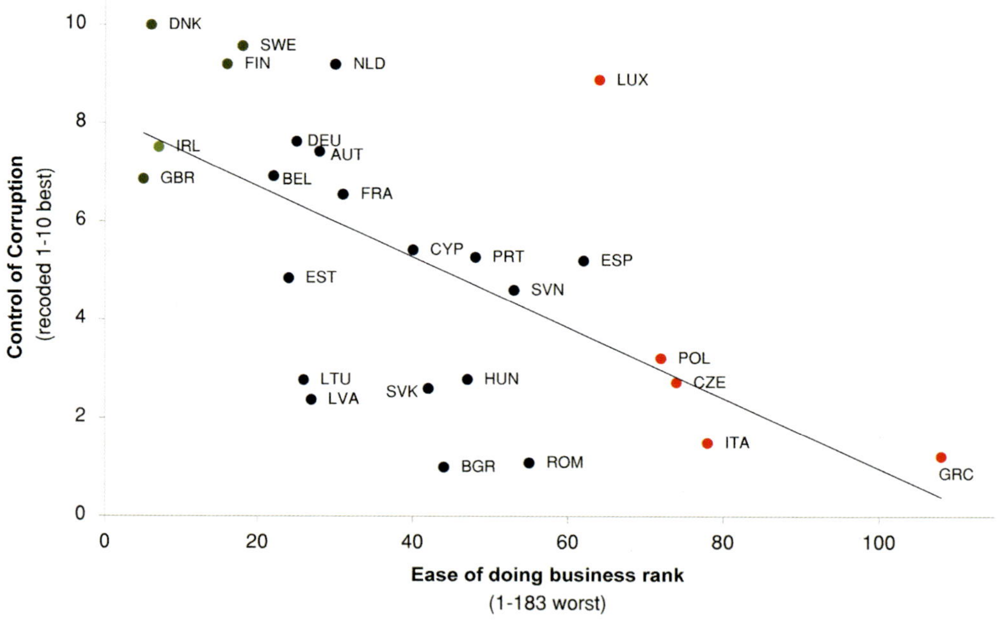

Data source: International Bank for Reconstruction and Development/World Bank, "Doing business 2010"

---

[14] The ease of doing business index provides a quantitative measure of regulations for starting a business, dealing with construction permits, employing workers, registering property, getting credit, protecting investors, paying taxes, trading across borders, enforcing contracts and closing a business – as they apply to domestic small and medium enterprises, available at <http://www.doingbusiness.org/reports/global-reports/doing-business-2010>

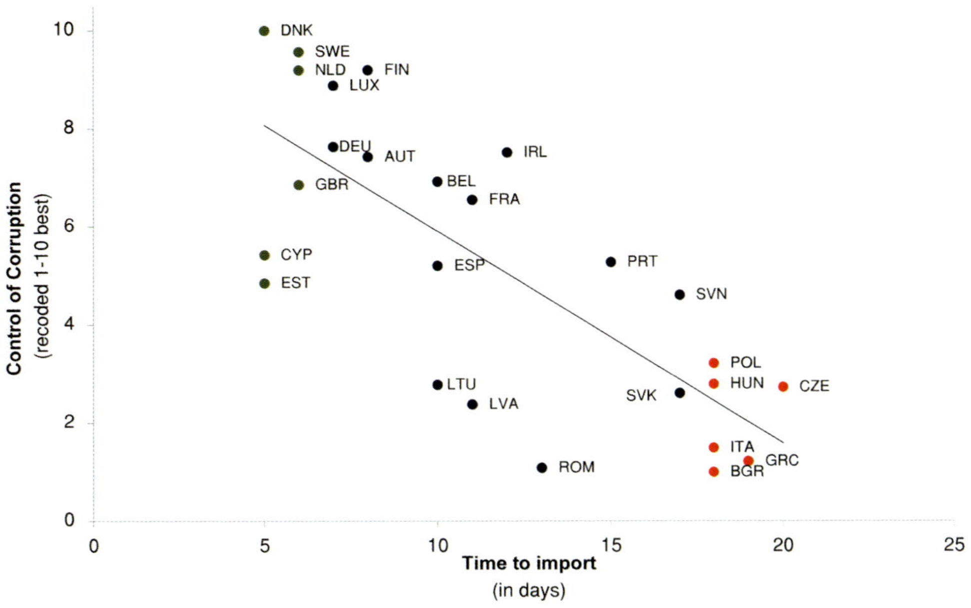

Data source: World Bank database. "Time to import (in days)"

2. **Transparency and e-government.** Transparency, in a variety of areas (fiscal transparency; transparency of assets for public officials; transparency of decision-making) is a key instrument for reducing administrative discretion. The more states offer their services electronically, the more corruption decreases (see **Figure 16** and **Figure 17**). The effect is however mediated by a population able to use such services, in other words connected to the Internet and using it. Italy, for instance, is a developed country with a reasonable number of Internet connections, but with limited use. New member countries like Estonia have curtailed corruption dramatically by cutting red tape and advancing e-government, practically eliminating most opportunities for corruption. Even in the absence of mass usage, transparency works due to mass media, NGOs or directly interested parties (for instance in procurement).

---

[15] Time to import in days is recorded in calendar days. The time calculation for a procedure starts from the moment it is initiated and runs until it is completed. If a procedure can be accelerated for an additional cost, the fastest legal procedure is chosen. It is assumed that neither the exporter nor the importer wastes time and that each commits to completing each remaining procedure without delay. Procedures that can be completed in parallel are measured as simultaneous. The waiting time between procedures –for example, during unloading of the cargo – is included in the measure, available at <http://data.worldbank.org/indicator/IC.IMP.DURS>

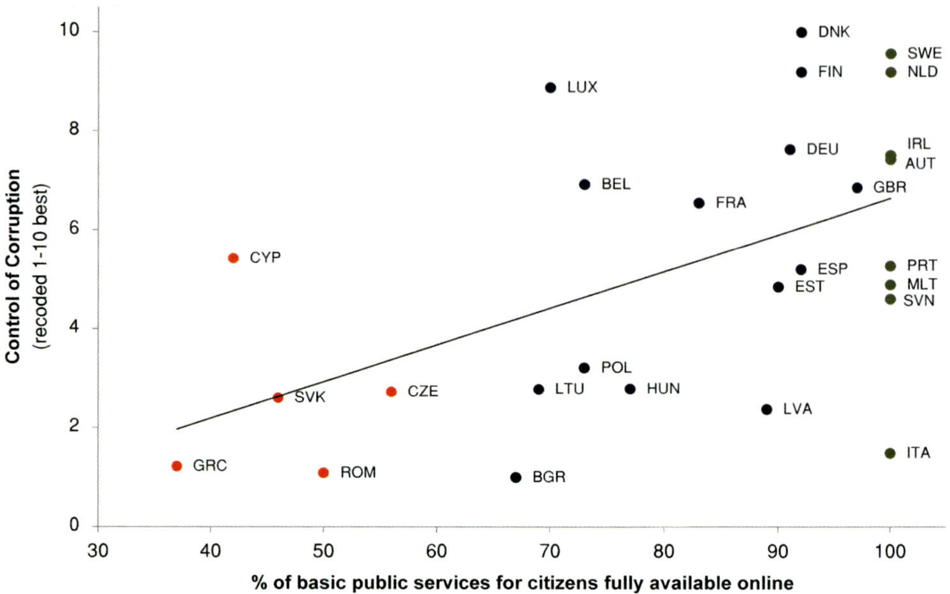

Data source: Capgemini, IDC, Rand Europe, Sogeti and DTi for the European Commission, Directorate General for Information Society and Media, "Digitizing Public Services in Europe: Putting ambition into action", 9th Benchmark Measurement, December 2010

---

[16] Extent to which there is a fully automated and proactive delivery of the 20 key public services. The 20 services used as reference for benchmarking are: income taxes, job search services, social security benefits (unemployment benefits, child allowances, medical costs, student grants), personal documents (passports, driving licence), car registration, application for building permission, declaration to the police, public libraries (catalogues, search tools), birth (and marriage) certificates, enrolment in higher education, announcement of moving, health-related services, social contribution for employees, corporate tax, VAT, registration of a new company, submission of data to statistical offices, customs declaration, environment related permits and public procurement, available at <http://www.capgemini.com/insights-and-resources/by-publication/2010-egovernment-benchmark>

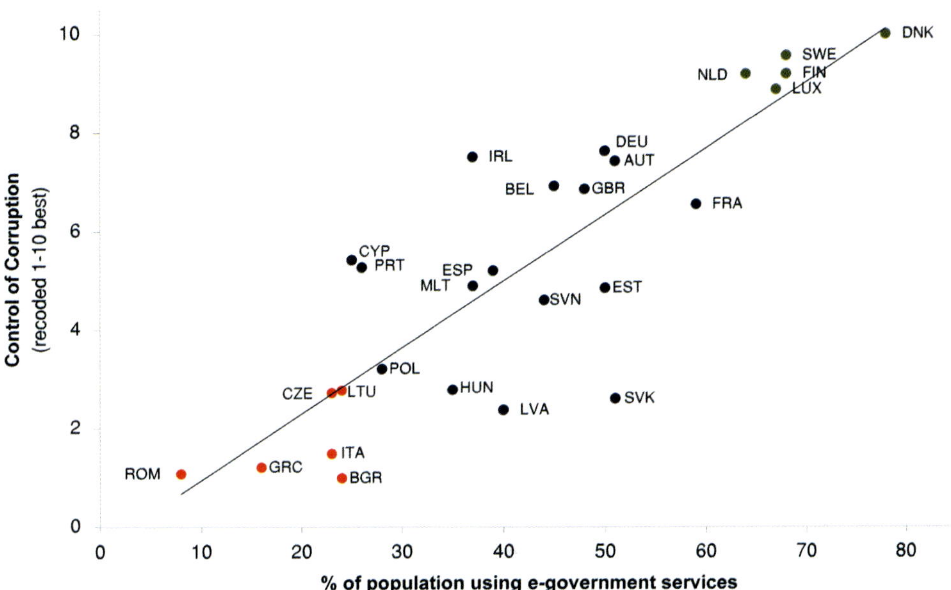

Data source: Capgemini for European Commission Directorate General for Information Society and Media, "The User Challenge Benchmarking: The Supply of Online Public Services – Seventh Measurement", 2007

3. Quality of audit for the public sector. Though we miss an objective evaluation of public sector audit, we have a measure of its effectiveness in the World Economic Forum's Global Competitiveness Report 2010-2011. This measure correlates very well with control of corruption (see **Figure 18**).

---

[17] Capgemini 2007: "The User Challenge Benchmarking The Supply Of Online Public Services – Seventh Measurement", prepared for the European Commission Directorate General for Information Society and Media, available at <http://www.de.capgemini.com/m/de/tl/EU_eGovernment_Report_2007.pdf>

Figure 18. Strength of auditing/reporting standards and corruption[18]

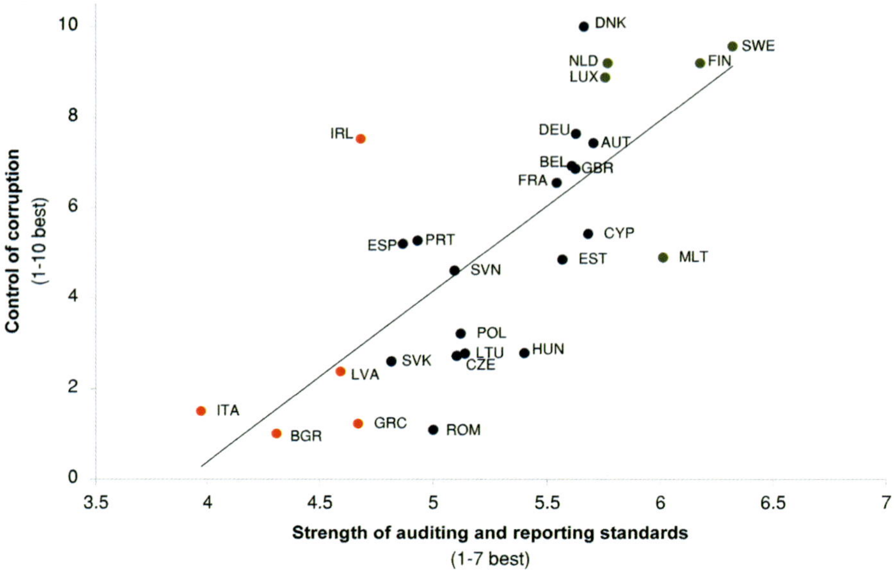

Data source: World Economic Forum, "Global Competitiveness Report 2010-2011"

4. **The dimension of public sector wages.** Development matters. Poverty and an informal economy are major corruption resources before themselves becoming impediments to development. Any country where claimants are in poverty, Court clerks discontented and income disparities great is unable to establish a judiciary capable of enforcing the law impartially and controlling corruption. Whilst we find a direct correlation between public sector wages and control of corruption (see **Figure 19**), we also find that it is overall development which matters and not just salaries in selected categories. In the EU as well as in the rest of the world it is easier to maintain adequate control of corruption if everyone concerned is reasonably comfortably off: policemen, judges, Court clerks, politicians and citizens. Presently, countries which pay law enforcers and judges more are not less corrupt, but rather the opposite (see **Figure 20**). This is probably because of the frequent reforms happening in corrupt countries. What is needed is a gradual and uniform rise in salaries, not disproportionate rises in certain public sector wages.

---

[18] Weighted average of the answers to the question: how would you assess financial auditing and reporting standards regarding company financial performance? Responses range from 1 (extremely weak) to 7 (extremely strong), available at <http://www3.weforum.org/docs/WEF_GlobalCompetitivenessReport_2010-11.pdf>

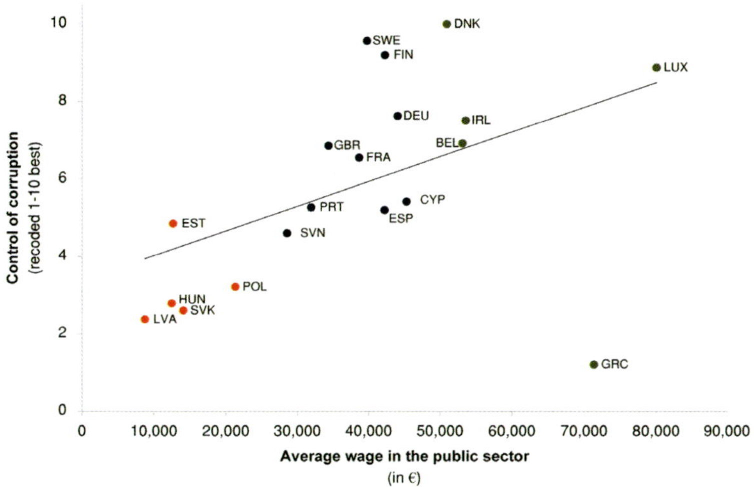

Data source: European Commission, Annual macro-economic database (AMECO)
and International Labour Organization, Laborsta database

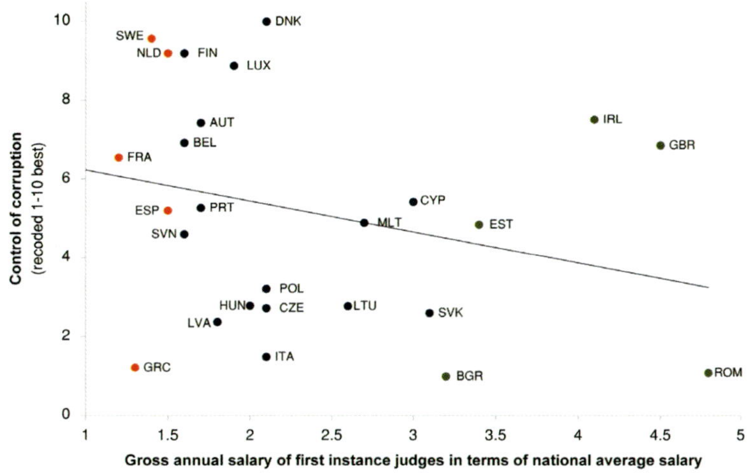

Data source: European Commission for the Efficiency of Justice,
"European Judicial Systems"

---

[19] Own estimation of average salaries in the public sector (in €), based on government expenditure on compensation of employees, available at <http://ec.europa.eu/economy_finance/db_indicators/ameco> and general government employment, available at <http://laborsta.ilo.org/default.html>. Data is from 2010, with the following exceptions: Hungary (2009), Greece, Portugal and Sweden (2007), and France (2006).

[20] Gross annual salary of 1st instance judges with regards to the national average gross annual salary. Data for the United Kingdom is based on the average of salaries in England, Wales and Scotland only, available at <http://www.coe.int/t/dghl/cooperation/cepej/evaluation/2012/Rapport_en.pdf>

5. **Civil society organizations (CSO) and the capacity for collective action.**
Control of corruption is significantly better in countries with a larger number
of CSOs (see **Figure 21**) and with more citizens engaged in voluntary activities
(see **Figure 22**). It does not matter what kind of CSOs nor what kind of voluntary activity, for as long as the capacity for association and collective action
exists a society is able to keep a check on public corruption. The association is so
strong that its contrary must be just as well understood. In the absence of public
oversight it is quite impossible even by repressive or administrative means to
build-in control of corruption. Again, that shows the disadvantage of some East
European and Mediterranean regions, which are rural and poor and have few
NGOs which are all based in cities anyway.

Figure 21. CSOs and corruption[21]

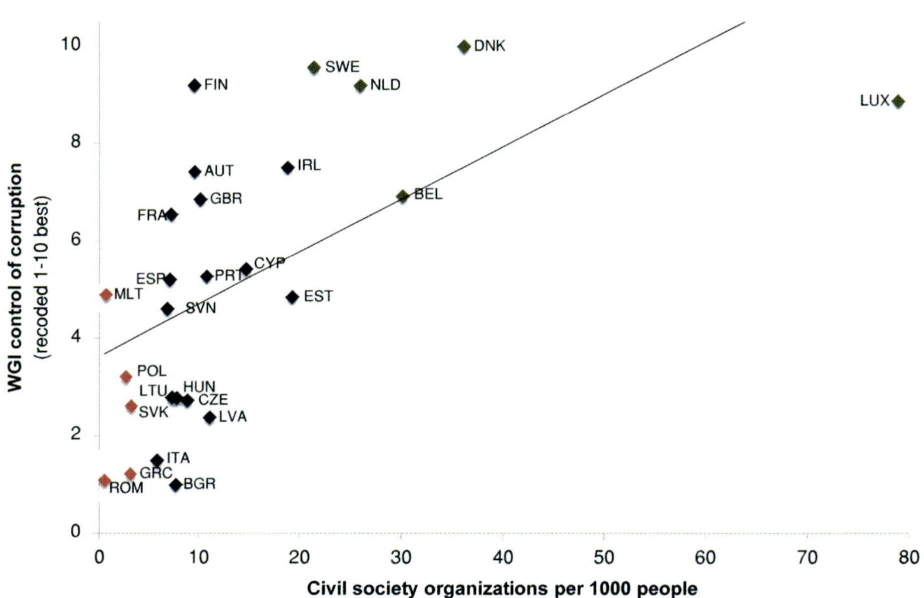

Data source: Quality of Government standard dataset

---

[21] Number of CSOs per million inhabitants, available at <http://www.qog.pol.gu.se/data/datadownloads/>

Figure 22. Voluntary work and corruption[22]

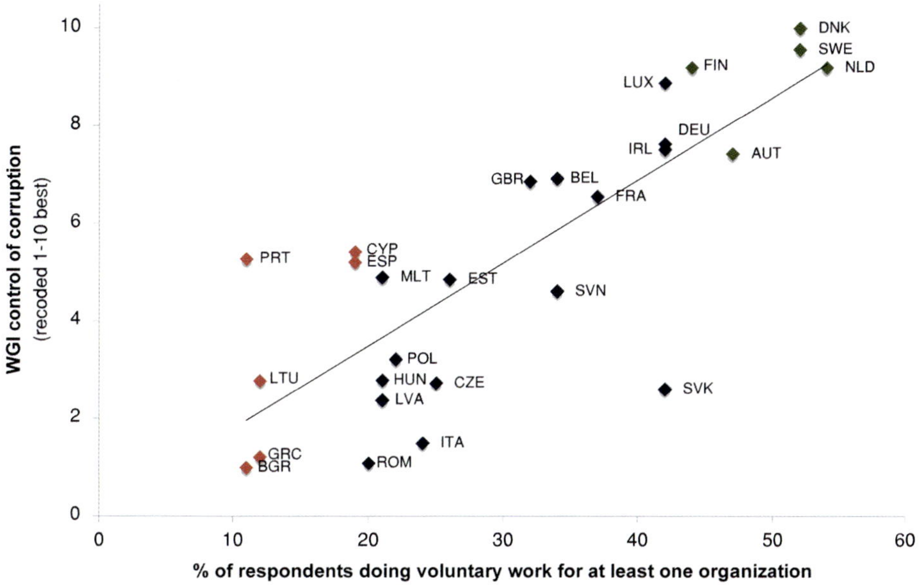

Data source: Standard Eurobarometer 72

6. Free media and well informed critical citizens. Freedom of media and the presence of a large number of citizens well-informed through newspapers or high Internet use explain in considerable part good control of corruption (See **Figure 23, Figure 24** and **Figure 25**). Knowledge of levels of newspaper readership and of use of the Internet enables us to predict the corruption score in over three quarters of European countries showing the extent to which a society's control of corruption is dependent on public scrutiny and the society's capacity for monitoring its own government.

---

[22] % of respondents that answered Yes to the question: QE 11. Do you currently participate actively in or do voluntary work for one or more of the following organisations? The organisations included in the list were: sports club or association, cultural, education or artistic association, charitable or social aid organisation, religious organisation, trade union, organisation for environmental protection, leisure association for the elderly, business or professional organisation, political party or organisation, interest groups for specific causes, international organisation, organisation defending the interests of patients and/or disabled people, consumer organisation, and organisation for the defence of the rights of elderly people.

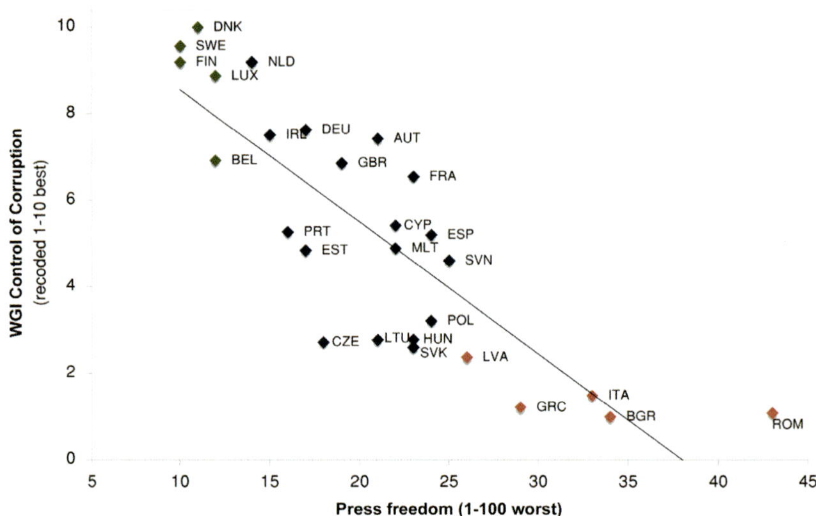

Figure 23. Freedom of the press and corruption[23]

Data source: Freedom House

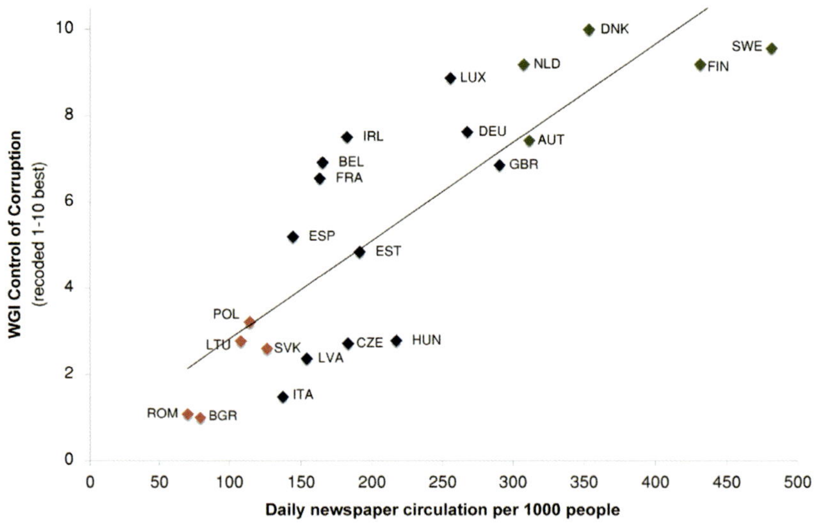

Figure 24. Newspaper readership and corruption[24]

Data source: World Bank database

---

[23] The press freedom index is computed by adding three component ratings: Laws and regulations, political pressures and controls and economic influences. The scale ranges from 0 (most free) to 100 (least free), available at <http://www.freedomhouse.org/report-types/freedom-press>

[24] Daily newspapers refer to those published at least four times a week and calculated as average circulation (or copies printed) per 1,000 people, available at <http://data.worldbank.org/indicator/IT.PRT.NEWS.P3>

Figure 25. Internet users and corruption[25]

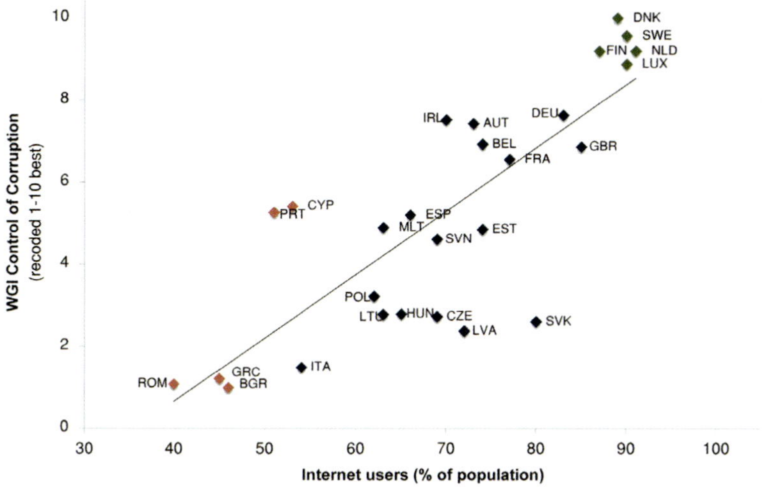

Data source: World Bank database

What seems to make no significant impact:

1. **Party funding restrictions**. In the European Union, leaving aside the countries which fund parties exclusively from the national budget we find that the more restrictions a country has on party funding the more corrupt it is. That indicates that countries which have achieved good control of corruption have managed it by other means, while those which struggle with corruption and address it with more and more legislation do not make much headway. In fact, except for the radical measure of banning private party financing altogether, we find no evidence that it works. Transparency of party funding, not type of party funding seems to matter more.

2. **Existence of a dedicated anticorruption agency.** Countries in the EU with special anticorruption agencies do not perform significantly better than countries which deal with corruption through their normal legal system. We do find a strong association between independence of the judiciary (expert score of WEF executive survey) and control of corruption. In other words, if the judiciary is independent from government, corruption can be controlled through normal prosecution and the Law Courts. If the judiciary is not independent, than an anticorruption agency is likely to become the target of political control, as has occurred in Latvia or Romania. In Slovenia, the battle for the agency was so fierce that a former head of it who was an internationally renowned anticorruption fighter was charged on petty administrative grounds when he left office.

3. **The existence of a Judicial Council.** In the EU, the existence of a Judicial Council entrusted with the self-regulation of magistrates is not associated with

---

[25] Internet users are people with access to the worldwide network, available at <http://data.worldbank.org/indicator/IT.NET.USER.P2>

any significantly better control of corruption. EU countries which have succeeded in building very effective control of corruption in Europe have done so by means of different institutional arrangements for their systems of prosecution and their judiciary arrangements. The one thing common to all – permanent positions for judges - was already in place throughout the EU. No other silver bullets in terms of the macro-organization of the judiciary can be found within the existing data.

IV. Evaluating corruption risks

Reviewing the performance of individual countries on the determinants of corruption sketched above (see **Annex 1** and **Annex 2** for the details) allows a better understanding of variations across Europe - beyond the obvious dichotomy between Scandinavia and the Eastern Balkans which is mirrored by a severe difference in development between the two European regions. We ranked the countries from best to worst performance by indicator using those proved to have a strong impact on corruption, and we calculated the EU27 averages and identified whether a country was above or below average, or in the bottom five. We then scored the position of each country, added up the individual scores across indicators[26] and grouped the results in the **Table 1**.

Table 1. EU countries by corruption risk group

		Resources/opportunities		
		Low		High
	Austria	Ireland		Cyprus
	Belgium	Luxembourg		Estonia
High	Denmark	Malta		Hungary
	Finland	Netherlands		Lithuania
	France	Sweden		
	Germany	United Kingdom		
	Italy			Bulgaria
	Portugal			Czech Republic
Low	Slovakia			Greece
	Slovenia			Latvia
	Spain			Poland
				Romania

(Row-label column at far left, rotated: **Deterrents /Constraints**, spanning High and Low.)

---

[26] Scores were assigned to each country depending on their ranking. For resources, we assigned 0 points to the best performers (above/below EU27 average depending on the indicator), 1 point to the middle group and 2 points to the bottom 5, since higher resources are associated with more corruption. For constraints, we assigned 2 points to the best performers (above/below EU27 average depending on the indicator), 1 point to the middle group and 0 to the bottom 5, since higher constraints are associated with less corruption. We then added the number of points obtained by each country and placed countries that obtained half or more of the available points in the resources or constraints indicators in the "high" category and those that obtained less than half the points in the "low" category.

The results enable us to classify all EU member states into four categories of corruption risk based on the causal model presented in the previous section.

Group A (high deterrents, low opportunities) is the group with the lowest risk of corruption, where control of corruption has been largely achieved and occasional corrupt acts can be dealt with successfully. It includes countries such as Austria, Belgium, Denmark, Finland, France, Germany, Ireland, Luxembourg, Malta, the Netherlands, Sweden and the UK. Those countries control opportunities for corruption through a transparent administration and economy, reduced officialdom and few opportunities for discretionary spending. Their equilibrium was arrived at via different historical paths and different organizational arrangements. Their diversity is good and the EU should not aspire to institutional 'monocropping'; in other words legislative arrangements and organization which are too similar across member states.

For countries struggling to build control of corruption the lessons from Group A countries are important insofar as they should be understood as development lessons. In other words, imports of current institutional arrangements from Group A countries to those with problems might be a tempting idea but is not likely to yield good results. What is crucial is rather to understand how the better-governed countries established control of corruption when corruption became a problem for them, in other words, their historical strategies for solving the problem. Institutions in current Group A countries are there for the maintenance rather than the establishing of control over corruption, and it is the latter that countries with problems need. None of the new member countries apart from Malta has managed to enter Group A, showing that there are still challenges for the control of corruption.

It must be mentioned, however, that control of corruption applies only within national borders; it is a domestic affair and nothing guarantees that a company from a country belonging to Group A when operating in another county where corruption is widespread would not play by the rules of the game applicable in countries where there is no control of corruption and outsiders might be obliged to pay bribes to enter particular markets. The only solution to that is strict enforcement of competition rules and monitoring of government favouritism within the EU.

Group B includes countries which have managed to create significant deterrents but still struggle with important challenges due to high resources for corruption. They include Estonia, Lithuania, Hungary and Cyprus. It might come as a surprise that a country like Estonia which performed best among new member countries and actively tries to reduce its resources for corruption through neoliberal and e-government policies is in this group. Two variables show the challenges remaining for control of corruption there, namely the presence of significant EU funds, which increases the risk of corruption; and of an informal economy. In this group Lithuania presents most challenges: a large informal economy and poor e-government combined with significant funds, both from domestic and EU sources, which all raise the risk. Hungary has low e-government and significant discretionary funds, mostly from EU sources. Meanwhile, poor e-government is the main risk for Cyprus.

Group C includes countries with relatively low resources, but low constraints too. This group is composed of three Mediterranean countries, Italy, Spain and Portugal; and two East European countries, Slovenia and Slovakia. The crisis has acted as a strong anticorruption agent in these countries, drying up resources and opportunities for corruption, yet they remain at higher risk than the previous group due to the presence of insufficient constraints. Moreover, normative social constraints and legal deterrents seem closely linked. The capacity to audit and control is considered insufficient in these countries; the independence of the judiciary is seen as problematic at least in Italy and Slovakia, and the tools available to society to control the government are feeble, with low levels of Internet connection (Spain and Slovenia do somewhat better), weak civil society and little media capacity to confront corruption.

Group D presents the highest corruption risks as it unites many opportunities with few deterrents. This group includes Greece from the old member states and five newer members: Poland, the Czech Republic, Latvia, Bulgaria and Romania, with control of corruption decreasing in that order. For a country to be in this group it must score among the five worst EU performers. Bulgaria, for example, on the constraints side scores lowest on audit capacity and judicial independence, as well as media freedom. On the opportunities side it is also in the bottom five for informal economy and discretionary funds. Romania is equally problematic, doing worst for the chapters of informal economy, discretionary spending, poor civil society, poor judiciary and it has a captive media and low internet access and little e-government. Greece combines a great deal of red-tape and low transparency with a poor performance overall on all constraints, legal and societal. Greek internet access and e-government are at the level of an underdeveloped country, while the country has an audit and a judiciary ranked among the worst. Civil society and media, in other words the demand for good governance are also at the level of the bottom five. Latvia has poor auditing and a captive media, as well as leading the European field for informal economy. It has significant EU funds though, which poses great risks. The Czech Republic's main risk is the presence of too much officialdom in combination with high levels of discretionary funds, which poses a challenge to the judiciary, and mediocre public financial control. Poland has high spending on projects combined with much red-tape and poorly developed civil society. The latter two countries do better than the rest in this group and are closer to Slovakia and Hungary, but they are not quite equal yet.

This comparative report shows considerable variation on control of corruption across EU member countries and opens the way to contextual reform paths for each and every country. Within each category of factors described here, specific strategies can be designed for each country based on the existing problems, but also the strengths of each country. As the statistical model presented here accounts for over 80% of the variation, so remedial work based on any of the factors presented above would be a substantial contribution to the control of corruption in the European Union.

Annex 1: OLS analysis for Control of Corruption (2010) with different resources as explaining variables

VARIABLES	(1) Model I	(2) Model II	(3) Model III	(4) Model IV	(5) Model V	(6) Model VI	(7) Model VII	(8) Model VIII	(9) Model IX	(10) Model X
Size of informal economy (% of GDP)	-0.23***	-0.13*								
	(0.044)	(0.059)								
Government investment in gross capital formation (% of GDP)			-0.93*	0.05						
			(0.449)	(0.401)						
Average public sector wages					0.00*	0.00				
					(0.000)	(0.000)				
Average annual regional and cohesion funds as % of GDP (2007-2013)							-1.55***	-0.85		
							(0.289)	(0.462)		
First instance judges salary ratio to national average salary									-0.78	0.13
									(0.541)	(0.432)
HDI score		31.28*		52.60***		49.56**		29.14		53.17***
		(13.015)		(11.630)		(16.773)		(15.397)		(10.826)
Constant	10.70***	-18.44	8.33***	-39.84**	3.39*	-37.18*	7.27***	-18.53	7.02***	-40.45***
	(1.118)	(12.168)	(1.587)	(10.717)	(1.230)	(13.769)	(0.539)	(13.640)	(1.344)	(9.714)
Observations	27	27	27	27	19	19	27	27	27	27
R-squared	0.52	0.61	0.15	0.54	0.22	0.50	0.53	0.59	0.08	0.54
Adj. R-squared	0.50	0.58	0.11	0.50	0.18	0.43	0.52	0.56	0.04	0.50

Standard errors in parentheses

*** p<0.001, ** p<0.01, * p<0.05

Annex 1 (cont.): OLS analysis for Control of Corruption (2010)
with different resources as explaining variables

VARIABLES	(11) Model XI	(12) Model XII	(13) Model XIII	(14) Model XIV	(15) Model XV	(16) Model XVI	(17) Model XVII	(18) Model XVIII
Time to import (in days)	-0.43***	-0.32***						
	(0.075)	(0.057)						
Ease of doing business			-0.07***	-0.05***				
			(0.019)	(0.013)				
% of population using e-government services					0.13***	0.10***		
					(0.017)	(0.019)		
Online availability and delivery of 20 basic public services							0.08*	0.03
							(0.032)	(0.026)
HDI score		36.35***		43.88***		23.84**		47.13***
		(7.207)		(7.784)		(8.413)		(10.295)
Constant	10.23***	-22.18**	8.15***	-30.08***	-0.39	-19.36**	-1.11	-37.55***
	(0.941)	(6.460)	(0.878)	(6.807)	(0.763)	(6.725)	(2.734)	(8.216)
Observations	26	26	26	26	27	27	27	27
R-squared	0.58	0.80	0.38	0.74	0.72	0.79	0.18	0.56
Adj. R-squared	0.56	0.78	0.36	0.72	0.71	0.77	0.15	0.53

Standard errors in parentheses

*** p<0.001, ** p<0.01, * p<0.05

Annex 2: OLS analysis for Control of Corruption (2010) with different constraints as explaining variables

VARIABLES	(1) Model I	(2) Model II	(3) Model III	(4) Model IV	(5) Model V	(6) Model VI	(7) Model VII	(8) Model VIII
Press freedom	-0.31***	-0.23***						
	(0.040)	(0.044)						
Internet users			0.15***	0.11***				
			(0.023)	(0.028)				
Daily Newspaper circulation per capita					0.02***	0.01***		
					(0.003)	(0.004)		
% of population doing voluntary work							0.17***	0.12**
							(0.025)	(0.037)
HDI score		25.39**		26.19*		34.36**		20.30
		(8.474)		(10.052)		(9.036)		(12.444)
Constant	11.61***	-11.72	-5.53**	-24.64**	0.55	-26.99**	0.09	-15.84
	(0.893)	(7.826)	(1.654)	(7.484)	(0.835)	(7.271)	(0.826)	(9.799)
Observations	27	27	27	27	22	22	27	27
R-squared	0.70	0.78	0.64	0.72	0.68	0.82	0.65	0.68
Adj. R-squared	0.69	0.76	0.62	0.69	0.67	0.80	0.64	0.66

Standard errors in parentheses

*** p<0.001, ** p<0.01,*p<0.05

Annex 2 (cont.): OLS analysis for Control of Corruption (2010)
with different constraints as explaining variables

VARIABLES	(9) Model IX	(10) Model X	(11) Model XI	(12) Model XII	(13) Model XIII	(14) Model XIV
CSOs per population	0.11**	0.07**				
	(0.030)	(0.023)				
Judicial independence			2.15***	1.87***		
			(0.176)	(0.235)		
Strength of auditing and reporting standards					3.78***	2.75***
					(0.663)	(0.510)
HDI score		42.15***		12.50		36.53***
		(9.293)		(7.127)		(7.162)
Constant	3.63***	-31.75***	-5.12***	-14.41*	-14.73***	-40.48***
	(0.620)	(7.814)	(0.874)	(5.366)	(3.524)	(5.630)
Observations	26	26	27	27	27	27
R-squared	0.36	0.66	0.86	0.87	0.56	0.79
Adj. R-squared	0.33	0.63	0.85	0.86	0.55	0.77

Standard errors in parentheses

*** p<0.001, ** p<0.01,*p<0.05

References

Bayley, D.H. 1966: "The Effects of Corruption in a Developing Nation", *The Western Political Science Quarterly* 19(4): 719-32

Becker, G. & Stigler G. 1974: "Law Enforcement, Malfeasance, and the Compensation of Enforcers", *Journal of Legal Studies* 3, 1-19

Dreher, A, & Schneider, F. 2010: "Corruption and the shadow economy: an empirical analysis", *Public Choice, 144*(1), 215-238

Dwivedi, O. P. 1967: "Bureaucratic Corruption in Developing Countries", *Asian Survey, 17/4*: 245-253

Huntington, S. 1968: *Political Order in Changing Societies*, New Haven, Yale University Press

Kaufmann, Daniel 2010: "Can Corruption Adversely Affect Public Finances in Industrialized Countries?", available at <http://www.brookings.edu/research/opinions/2010/04/19-corruption-kaufmann>, last accessed Feb. 15, 2013

Klitgaard, Robert 1988: *Controlling Corruption*, Berkley CA: University of California Press
Leys, C. 1965: "What is the Problem About Corruption?" *Journal of Modern African Studies* 3(2): 215-24

Merton, Robert K. 1957: *Social Theory and Social Structure*, Free Press, Glencoe, Ill.

Mungiu-Pippidi, Alina et al. 2011: Contextual Choices in Fighting Corruption: Lessons Learned, NORAD, Report 4/2011, available at: <http://www.norad.no/en/tools-and-publications/publications/publication?key=383808>

Nye, J. S. 1967: "Corruption and Political Development: A Cost-Benefit Analysis", *American Political Science Review*, Vol. 61, No. 2: 417– 427

Rothstein, Bo & Uslaner, Eric M. 2005: "All for All: Equality and Social Trust," *World Politics*, 58 (October), 41-72

Strömberg, Håkan 2000: *Allmän Förvaltningsrätt*, Malmö: Liber

Sung, Hung-En 2003: "Fairer Sex or Fairer System? Gender and Corruption Revisited" *Social Forces 82(2): 703-723*

Van Rijckeghem, Caroline & Weder, Beatrice 1997: "Corruption and the Rate of Temptation: Do low Wages in the Civil Service cause Corruption?" *IMF Working Paper*

Warner, Carolyn 2007: *The Best System Money Can Buy: Corruption in the European Union*, Ithaca and London: Cornell University Press

3. The South-Eastern Europe

ALINA MUNGIU-PIPPIDI

When the promise to enlarge to the Western Balkans was issued at the Thessaloniki Summit in 2003 by EU leaders, democracy and rule of law were declared from the very first paragraph to be 'common values'. Strengthening the rule of law and public administration reform are acknowledged as key issues ten years later, after the successful accession of Croatia. The Council showed that it did not underestimate the challenge when stating that these 'issues should be tackled early in the enlargement process to allow the maximum time to establish the necessary legislation, institutions and solid track records of implementation before the negotiations are closed' [Council of the European Union, 2011].

This wisdom is grounded in the mixed experience of the big bang enlargement wave, and, in particular, the negative experience of Romania and Bulgaria, which years after accession are still struggling to meet the established criteria in these areas. But the challenges historically encountered by external 'civilising' empires in their attempts to transform the Balkans are much older. Describing such ventures by the ancient Greeks, historian Arnaldo Momigliano wrote: 'But the Greeks were seldom in a position to check what natives told them: they did not know the languages. The natives, on the other hand, being bilingual, had a shrewd idea of what the Greeks wanted to hear and spoke accordingly. This reciprocal position did not make for sincerity and real understanding' (Momiglian 1975: 8). Such anecdotes can still be found today. But also progress exists.

Since they started from so low a point after the wars that accompanied the breakup of the former Yugoslavia, the Balkan countries have actually progressed on average more than other regions in the world (except for the Caribbean) in terms of the World Bank Rule of Law and Control of Corruption index. **Figure 1** below shows the Western Balkan countries that have made statistically significant progress, compared with the only three new member countries which have managed the same. On a scale from one to 100, the most advanced, Estonia, is the only one in the upper quarter of good governance, having started from a far better position, but Croatia, Serbia and the former Yugoslav Republic of Macedonia (FYROM) have made significant progress when compared to their 1996 rankings and have come to overshadow Bulgaria and Romania. Croatia, the most advanced, hovers around the rank of sixty, which is where most 'borderline' cases in the world are situated. A borderline case is a fairly modern state where the main norm in public resource allocation is still 'particularism': in other words, nepotism and corruption are still the norm rather than the exception.

Figure 1. The Balkan achievers – significant changes in control of corruption in Eastern Europe (1996-2011)

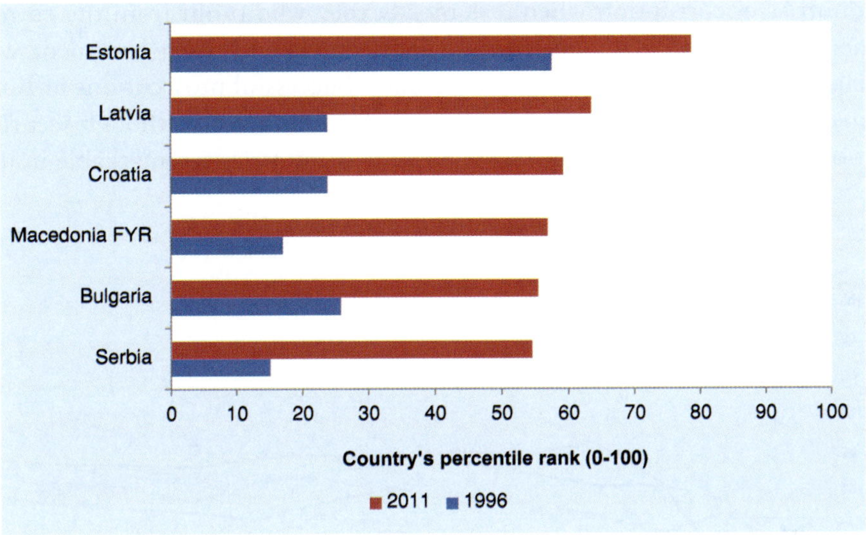

Data source: Worldwide Governance Indicators (1996-2011)

So these three Western Balkan countries can be seen as achievers, although they are still far from the good governance zone in the chart (above 70th percentile). Montenegro, although the youngest country, has performed similarly to FYROM and Serbia. News is less good concerning the other Western Balkan countries. Albania and Bosnia and Herzegovina have also progressed, but less.

Figure 2 shows how close all Balkan countries are. Slovenia is the positive outlier on top and Albania and Kosovo are the negative outliers on the bottom. This mirrors the difference in terms of economic development between the two extremes. The core group of countries presents few differences, and in fact share the same governance diagnosis. The main governance institutions do not vary from the Eastern to Western Balkans, amounting to regimes based on political pluralism where victory in elections means significant spoiling of the state by the winners, ranging from the allocation of public appointments (even at minor levels) to public contracts, concessions and privatisations. This regime is dominated by clientelism (taking the various forms of patronage, pork barrel spending and networks of influence-peddling). This behaviour is the rule of the game not only in politics, but also in many business areas, where the favouritism shown by the government to certain companies seriously distorts market competition. It also pervades other aspects of public life, for instance in universities. Open and fair competition is rare.

This is the standard portrait of all European countries ranked under the threshold of 60, with the exception of Bosnia and Herzegovina, where the dividing lines of client groups are of an ethnic rather than political party nature. This also means that law enforcement agencies and the judiciary are only partly effective, with a significant number of the powerful and privileged escaping their control. Nearly all elected politicians belong to the sphere of the privileged, many of whom feel threatened by the EU's stress on the rule of law and anticorruption measures, since this is how politics works. In other words, it is rather difficult to entrust political elites with the task of ridding their countries of corruption when it is mostly they who profit from the current arrangements: hence the low voter turnout in elections and disenchantment with all politicians in both Eastern and Western Balkans. Successful prosecutions in Romania and Croatia have not managed so far to have a deterrent effect, although securing the convictions of former prime ministers in these two countries is remarkable in itself.

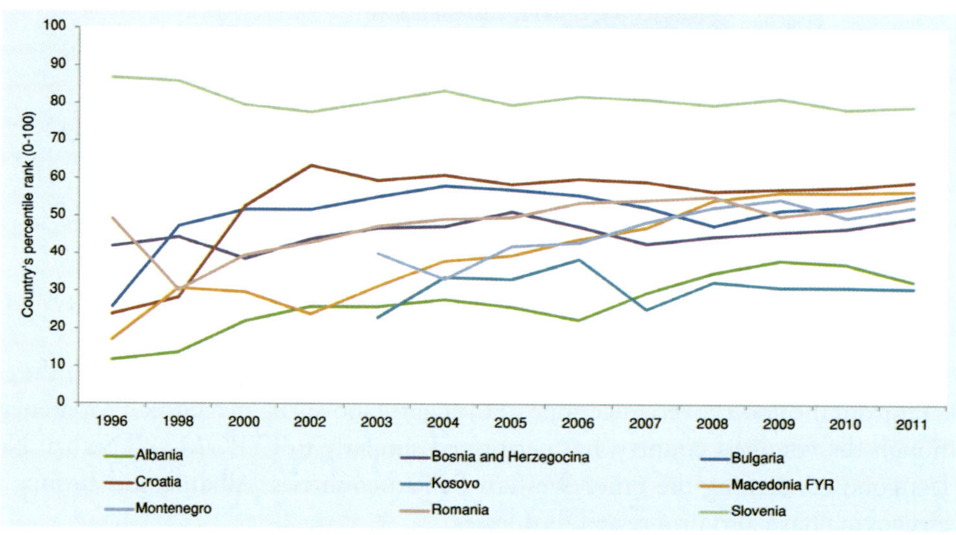

Figure 2. Control of corruption across the Eastern and Western Balkans (country's percentile rank 0-100)

Data source: Worldwide Governance Indicators (1996-2011)

The Western Balkan countries do not fare worse on governance than the average of their income group as classified by the World Bank. The individual country's level of development therefore matters significantly. Poverty and an informal economy are major drivers of corruption before themselves becoming impediments to development. Any country where claimants are in poverty, Court clerks discontented and income disparities great has difficulty establishing a judiciary capable of enforcing the law impartially and controlling corruption.

But how can effective control of corruption be achieved? Using the model described in the chapter 2 (on the methodology, see Mungiu-Pippidi et al. 2011) the main significant determinants of corruption are reviewed. The statistical tests employed (based on OLS regressions) essentially use a comparative method that makes it possible to evaluate whether countries which perform better are more or less associated with a certain determinant: the observations are either global (N=191) or European (N=27 or 40 if Southeastern European and European ex-Soviet Union countries are included). The following factors have a high impact and influence corruption greatly in the Western Balkans.

Resources and opportunities:

- **'Red tape'.** There is a very strong association between red tape and corruption, as excessive regulation is the main instrument used to increase administrative discretion and through it corruption. Streamlining regulation is not an objective during accession negotiations, so this issue is generally sidelined. On the contrary, regulations multiply without being properly implemented, thus magnifying the distance between norm and practice.

- **Transparency and e-government.** Transparency, in a variety of areas (fiscal expenditure; information regarding public officials' assets and decision-making processes) is a key instrument for reducing administrative discretion. The more states offer their services electronically, the more corruption decreases. This all however depends on the extent to which the population is able to use such services, in other words has free and generalised access to the internet. New member countries like Estonia have curtailed corruption dramatically by cutting red tape and advancing e-government, practically eliminating most opportunities for corruption. Even in the absence of mass internet usage, transparency works due to mass media, NGOs or directly interested parties (for instance in procurement). Unfortunately this issue is not addressed during the accession process. Only e-procurement is sometimes discussed, when transparency should be the cornerstone of all civil service, public administration and fiscal management reforms.

- **High spending with discretionary potential (projects).** On the European continent, the more leeway a government has for discretionary spending, the more it tends to be corrupt. It is not general spending which is correlated with corruption, but the funds that a government has the freedom to allocate discretionarily and that are not tied to some clear objective like social entitlements. Funds from foreign aid and state-owned natural resources also enter this category. This explains cases such as Kosovo, praised by the European Commission (EC) in its 2011 Progress Report for having introduced improvements in its procurement legislation. But further improvements would not help strengthen control of corruption in Kosovo as long as the value of public procurement contracts awarded yearly remains at around 20 percent of Kosovo's GDP, about €482 million (US$645 million for 2009, according to estimates by Global Integrity Report). The EU accession process here unwittingly introduces new opportunities for corruption due to the influx of EU funds, which can be discretionarily spent by the governments, either directly or by manipulating national matching funds.

Constraints and deterrents:

- **Quality of audit for the public sector.** Although no objective evaluation of public sector audits exists as such, the World Economic Forum's (WEF) Global Competitiveness Report 2010-2011 offers an expert assessment of the effectiveness of public sector audits. This measure correlates very well with control of corruption. The quality of control and preventive measures in general is under-emphasised during the EU accession process and in the Mechanism for Cooperation and Verification (MCV) for Romania and Bulgaria, a safeguard clause allowing the

European Commission to check on the status of their prior commitments in the field of rule of law even after accession.

- **Civil society and the capacity for collective action.** Regression analysis shows that control of corruption is significantly better in countries with a larger number of NGOs and with more citizens engaged in voluntary activities. The correlation is so strong that its reverse is self-evident: in the absence of public oversight, it is quite impossible to achieve effective control of corruption. During the accession process some funds are earmarked to help civil society in general, but no systematic effort has been made to create a civil society watchdog and mechanism for monitoring spending of EU funds, for instance, although this would prevent waste, provide a timely alert regarding incidents of corruption and contribute to the more effective use of such funds.

- **Free media and well-informed critical citizens.** Freedom of the media and the presence of a large number of well-informed citizens with regular access to newspapers or access to the internet explain in considerable part the successful control of corruption. Knowledge of the levels of newspaper readership and use of the Internet enables us to predict the corruption score in over three quarters of European countries showing the extent to which a society's control of corruption is dependent on public scrutiny and the society's capacity for monitoring its own government. The European Commission (EC) and the Council both noticed that problems affecting freedom of expression and the media remain a particular concern but except for monitoring developments no real remedies were found. These would include encouraging local governments to support the new media, which are less prone to capture by vested interests, and invest in developing the media's capacity to play the role of good governance watchdog.

The following factors seem to make less significant statistical impact:

- **Party funding restrictions**. In Europe, leaving aside the countries which fund parties exclusively from the national budget, the more restrictions a country has on party funding, the more corrupt it seems to be according to regression analysis. It may be because these countries adopted restrictions in recent years to fight political corruption, but the evidence also shows that countries which have achieved good control of corruption have managed it with different party funding arrangements. In short, the only existing statistical evidence available so far shows that transparency of sources of party funding has some deterrent effect on political corruption. It is more useful to constrain the capacity of political parties to favour companies with public contracts, which are easy to monitor, than to be continually endeavouring to improve party funding legislation, where more restrictions frequently result in more illegal or intricately arranged transfers. If parties cannot deliver to their sponsors, the latter will freeze the money themselves.

- **Existence of a dedicated anticorruption agency.** Countries in Europe with special prosecuting anticorruption agencies do not perform significantly better than countries which deal with corruption through their normal judiciary. In other words, if the judiciary is independent from government, corruption can be controlled through normal prosecution procedures and the law courts (prosecutors can in any case undergo specialised training in this field). If the judiciary is not independent, then an 'autonomous' anticorruption agency risks becoming a target for political control, as has already occurred in Slovenia, Latvia or Romania. However, the EC has taken the line that corruption can be controlled through these special agencies, despite evidence that agencies alone cannot cope with the problem if all other policy factors are not addressed. The result is a situation as in Romania in 2009-2012 when corruption worsened while the anticorruption agency performed better and better and received high praise in EU reports.

- **Existence of a Judicial Council.** Neither globally nor in Europe is the existence of a Judicial Council entrusted with the self-regulation of magistrates associated with a more effective control of corruption. EU countries which have historically succeeded in achieving effective control of corruption in Europe have done so by means of different institutional arrangements for their systems of prosecution and Courts. Since their adoption the judiciary has indeed been less subject to direct political intervention, but indirect influence, and especially corruption, remain rife. In many countries the judiciary has become plainly unaccountable since judges have started to rule themselves. Global Integrity reports for instance that, in Albania, Court positions at different levels have in recent years acquired a price tag.

The evidence that the EU enlargement process, despite the stress on anticorruption, is having a hard time delivering can be explained by an indicator developed by Global Integrity which reports on both the 'legal framework' and 'implementation' separately, allowing a measurement of the 'implementation gap'. The results available for the past couple of years show that all Western Balkan countries have improved to reach either a very strong (e.g. Kosovo) or strong legal framework, with weak or very weak (e.g. Serbia) implementation. This shows that the gap between formal rules and their actual implementation only grew, with little impact on corruption so far and suggests that rather than new improvements of laws better enforcement of existing legislation should be stressed.

Table 1 shows the most important factors determining control of corruption. Freedom House's Nations in Transit project evaluates that the judiciary has not evolved in any country in the Western Balkans except for a small improvement in Kosovo (0.25, the smallest unit of progress) in the last five years. The media, which plays an essential role in scrutinizing government and informing the public, has weakened in the last few years, ending up captured by vested interests, and thus becoming useless as an accountability tool. Civil society is still numerically reduced and demoralised, with scarce funds for the monitoring of good governance. These three areas – empowerment of the media and civil society and promotion of fiscal transparency (with, as the Open Budget Index shows, poor performance across countries) – might be the best investment for the EU, at least to diminish the risk induced by the accession process itself, if not to radically change the governance regime of the region.

Table 1. The Western Balkans governance indicators

	Albania	Bosnia	Croatia	Kosovo	FYROM	Montenegro	Serbia
WEF bribery rank (144 countries)	84	63	91		53	54	86
WEF government favouritism rank (144 countries)	84	70	97		77	31	132
WEF judicial independence rank (144 countries)	121	78	106		105	65	129
Nations in Transit Press freedom (1-7 worst) Evolution over the last five years	4.00 (0)	4.75 (-0.5)	4.00 (-0.25)	5.75 (-0.25)	4.75 (0.75)	4.00 (-0.5)	4.25 (-1)
Global Integrity implementation gap index (1-100)	21	-	-	31	30	-	30
Open Budget Index (1-100)	47	50	61	-	35	-	39
Size of shadow economy as % of GDP (2007)	37.7	35.4	36.5	-	38.8	-	-
Ease of doing business rank (132 countries)	85	126	84	98	23	51	86

Source: author's compilation. All figures are from 2012 unless otherwise indicated.

The EU could also consider the cases of Romania and Bulgaria alongside that of Croatia. The EU tried to rise to the challenge in these two countries, by using to an unprecedented degree the Mechanism of Cooperation and Verification (MCV), tied to progress on corruption in both countries, and the temporary freezing of EU funds until better governance arrangements were also put in place. These negative experiences of the unfinished Eastern Balkans governance transformations weigh heavily on the forecast for the Western Balkans accession process. All parties concerned would do well to draw lessons learned from this experience – in particular the EU, which seems sometimes to be pursuing a strategy in the Western Balkans that is not so different from that with which it previously experimented in Romania and Bulgaria.

References

Momigliano, Arnaldo. 1975: Alien Wisdom. The Limits of Hellenization, Cambridge: Cambridge University Press.
Mungiu-Pippidi, Alina et al. 2011: Contextual Choices in Fighting Corruption: Lessons Learned, NORAD, Report 4/2011, available at: <http://www.norad.no/en/tools-and-publications/publications/publication?key=383808>

4. The Former Soviet Union

ROXANA BRATU

This report analyses efforts to control corruption in twelve countries of the Former Soviet Union (FSU), namely Belarus, Moldova, Ukraine, Armenia, Georgia, Azerbaijan, Kazakhstan, Kyrgyzstan, Tajikistan, Turkmenistan, Uzbekistan and Russia. It argues that despite a general trend towards the augmentation of anti-corruption interventions, national contexts each show different degrees of integration between global anti-corruption and local enforcements. The evidence indicates tensions between internationally-led policies and local practices.

Introduction

Over the past decade corruption has become *the* major challenge that FSU countries have had to face in their journey towards modernisation. Despite numerous anti-corruption interventions, a growing industry of consultants, programmes and funding packages, the region continues to display rather ambiguous trends. According to Transparency International's 2012 report, nearly all the countries in this region fall below the global average (Georgia is the exception). The similar World Bank Control of Corruption shows countries in the region below the level of sub-Saharan Africa, the least developed part of the world (see **Figure 1**). Within the region, only four countries are above the regional average, with Georgia the anti-corruption champion, followed by Armenia, Moldova and Belarus (see **Figure 2**). These measurements have certain limitations that we are ware of (Knack 2006; Galtung 2005).

Figure 1. Regional trends of corruption control

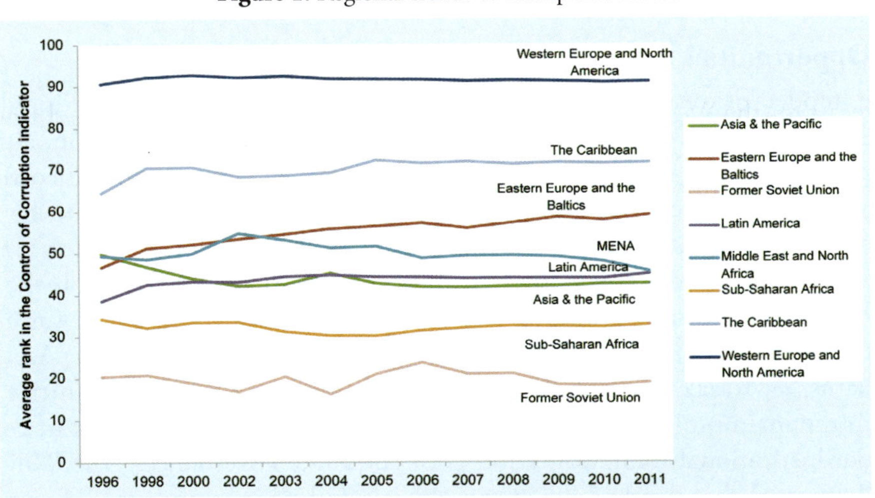

Source: Control of Corruption, Worldwide Governance Indicators, Regional mean 1996-2011

This paper offers a qualitative review of anti-corruption interventions in the region. It is based on secondary data such as: monitoring reports provided by major international institutions, implementation documents, regional research papers, newspaper articles and various ranking/measurement indexes (provided by World Bank, Transparency International, Freedom House, etc.). In order to ensure the validity and reliability of the material, the sources were cross-checked and data used if it was mentioned by more than two reliable sources. A full list of sources used as footnotes is available online at www.anticorrp.eu, this print version being an abridged version of the original material.

In order to trace anti-corruption initiatives, the paper is organised into three main sections. The first section discusses the opportunities and resources for corruption. The second section looks at its deterrents and the third section focuses on anti-corruption and its prospects.

Figure 2. Performance on control of corruption - Former Soviet Union

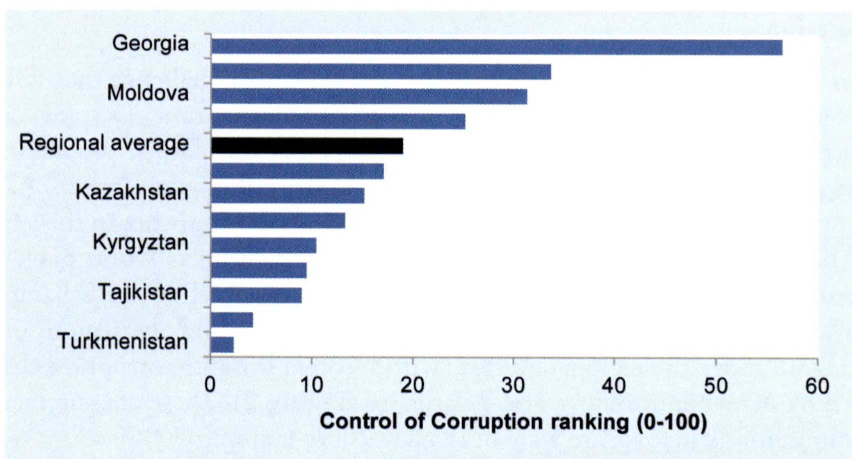

Source: Control of Corruption, Worldwide Governance Indicators, 2012

1. Opportunities and resources for corruption

The model of resources and constraints developed by Mungiu-Pippidi (see chapter 2) would indeed predict poor control of corruption in this region, although we register impressive developments at the level of legal constraints (anticorruption strategies). For instance, **red tape** and corruption of officials continue to be major challenges for business. The 2013 World Bank 'Ease of doing business' ranking shows incoherent development. By that measure, the higher the position the worst the economic environment; and of 185 economies ranked, Uzbekistan was at 154, Tajikistan 141, Ukraine 137, Russia 112, Moldova 83, Kyrgyzstan 70, Azerbaijan 67, Belarus 58, Kazakhstan 49, Armenia 32 and Georgia 9. For the countries at the bottom, the main problems are related to corruption, weak enforcement of contract law, poor institutional frameworks and poor corporate governance. The Wall Street Journal reported that nearly 33% of top officials and finance professionals suggested that corruption was a major hindrance to the Russian economy. The Moscow Times reports that 95% of surveyed businessmen feel that due to corruption, 'the current environment is not encouraging innovation and entrepreneurship'.

Such bleak perceptions might also be because the business climate is dominated by the **intrusion of government into business**, which is a major resource for corruption (Klitgaard 1988). Large state-run enterprises with heavy impact on national economies are a common factor. In Kazakhstan, Samruk-Kazyna controls more than half the national economy and manages the state assets in oil and gas, energy, transport, telecommunication, and the financial and innovation sectors. Moreover, it "has a pre-emptive right to buy strategic facilities and bankrupt assets. It is exempt from government procurement procedures ... has the right to establish its own procurement rules"[1]. In the face of such extraordinary powers, the private sector and foreign companies face serious obstacles. In Tajikistan, little effort has been made to increase the transparency of state owned enterprises, the ruling elite benefiting directly from enterprises such as the Tajik Aluminium Company (TALCO)[2]. According to Freedom House (2012), TALCO uses 40% of the country's electricity supply, and its production is sold through 'opaque' entities registered in the British Virgin Islands. A common practice is selling state property to close allies of the regime for an artificially low price. Sometimes the buyer is a company set up just days before the sale. In Georgia, "Geoland" LLC bought 8000 sq. m. of land in the Kazbegi Municipality, later sold for a nominal sum in November, 2012. It has been revealed that the brother of the mayor of Tbilisi, Irakli Ugulava, owns 50% of the shares of the company[3].

The great **mineral resources** of the region are a similarly important resource for corruption, as they provide a powerful incentive to the international community to overlook national problems with democracy and corruption, as well as offering a consistent source of rents for local elites. In Kazakhstan, US investment totalled $177.7 billion in September 2012 and the bulk of that was directed to the gas and oil sectors. In those sectors, corruption scandals involved internal actors, politicized actions and prestigious international economic entities. For instance, in November 2012 a senior Kyrgyz Energy Ministry official was accused of providing an operating licence to the company KasEnergo which had bought energy at a discount price and then sold it to the general public at a far higher price. The fraudulent scheme had an estimated value of 1.7 million Kyrgyzstan som (KGS) or $36,000[4]. Meanwhile, the government-owned Kazakh company KazMunaiGaz has decided to put red dye into diesel produced at the Pavlodar refinery. Bloomberg reports that the Pavlodar refinery will "colour 159,500 metric tons of the fuel ... destined to be sold"[5]. A high profile

---

[1] US Department of State. (2012). *Investment climate statement – Kazakhstan*. Available at: <http://www.state.gov/e/eb/rls/othr/ics/2012/191174.htm>

[2] US Department of State. (2013). *Investment Climate Statement – Tajikistan*. Available at: <http://photos.state.gov/libraries/tajikistan/231771/PDFs/2013-tajikistan-investment-climate-statement-final.pdf>

[3] Transparency International Georgia. (2013*). Illegally appointed municipality governors of Gurjaani and Dedoplistskaro*. Available at: <http://transparency.ge/en/blog/property-sold-gel-1-problematic-trends>

[4] Sultankulova, A. (2012). *Kyrgyzstan Energy Official Faces Corruption Charges*. RiaNovosti. Available at: <http://en.rian.ru/news/20121112/177388448.html>

[5] Gizitdinov, N. (2013). *Kazakh Refinery to Dye Diesel Red to Combat Embezzlement*. Bloomberg. Available at: <http://www.bloomberg.com/news/2013-03-15/kazakh-refinery-to-dye-diesel-red-to-combat-embezzlement.html>

scandal form Kazakhstan (Atyrau region) involved an estimated $100 million-worth of damage to the state budget, and the brother of the recently dismissed regional governor Bergey Ryskaliyev is under investigation for fraud. Sceptical observers suggest that this corruption scandal is "all part of a wider battle of Kazakhstan's … bickering clans" and not a 'genuine' corruption scandal[6].

Major international companies have also been linked with alleged corruption involving the Kazakh Customs Service. An international consortium, known as Tengrizchevroil, consisting of Chevron Corp., ExxonMobil Corp. and Deutsche Post AG's logistics business DHL opened an investigation into allegations that DHL bribed customs officials in Kazakhstan on behalf of the group. Allegedly, DHL paid "convoy bribes" on behalf of Tengizchevroil, in order to ensure that "escorts" did not delay the shipping of Tengizchevroil's equipment; the partnership's logistics agents regularly paid $150 to $300 in bribes to customs officials, which DHL then reimbursed[7]. Customs services in the region are reputedly corrupt: as recently as 2007 Global Integrity reported that $140 million in bribes were collected by Kazakh Customs.

Two more factors foster corruption in the region: ethnic conflicts and underground black economies. The realities of those factors on the ground have determined the policy makers to combine anti-corruption policies and aid packages with policies against drug-related crime, tax evasion and avoidance, security crime and terrorism. The conflict between Armenia and Azerbaijan over Nagorno Karabakh prompted military aid from the United States. Armenia received $600,000 and Azerbaijan $2,700,000, while Nagorno Karabakh as a de facto independent state received $5,000,000. The Georgian military service received $1,800,000 and $12,000,000 in 2013, probably in relation to the Georgia - Russia conflict of 2008 over South Osetia. The regional bilateral tension between Uzbekistan and Kyrgyzstan has been causing significant social and economic harm, as Kyrgyz nationalists suppressed the Uzbek population in Osh, and Uzbeks have begun to withdraw their business and assets from the region[8]. The Anti-Crime and Corruption Department Chief of the Kyrgyz Ministry was killed in Osh, his death allegedly caused for professional motives[9].

The NATO operation in Afghanistan prompted **substantial amounts of foreign aid in the region, another resource of corruption** reported in the literature (Ledeneva 2003). For example, Tajikistan and Kazakhstan received $355 million and $214 million according to OECD statistics. Because of a lack of proper oversight, in 2007 an investigation by the National Bank of Tajikistan revealed that the government had misused $310 million of aid[10]. There have been no major aid-related scandals since

---

[6] Lillis, J. (2012). *Kazakhstan: Corruption Scandal Engulfs Oil-Rich Western Region*. Eurasianet. Available at: <http://www.eurasianet.org/node/66019>

[7] Matthews, C. M. (2012). *Second Oil Venture Probes Corruption Allegations in Kazakhstan*. The Wall Street Journal Blogs Available at: <http://blogs.wsj.com/corruption-currents/2012/06/13/second-oil-venture-probes-corruption-allegations-in-kazakhstan/>

[8] USDOS. (2012). *Country reports on human rights practices. Secretary's Preface*. Available at: <http://www.state.gov/j/drl/rls/hrrpt/humanrightsreport/#wrapper>

[9] Ivashchenko, Y.(2013). *Kyrgyzstan: Anti-crime and corruption department chief shot dead in Osh*. Fergananews. Available at: <http://enews.fergananews.com/news.php?id=2448&mode=snews>

[10] Wickberg, S. (2013). *Overview of Corruption and Anti-corruption in Tajikistan*. U4 Anti-Corruption Resource Centre. Available at: <http://www.u4.no/publications/overview-of-corruption-and-anti-corruption-

then, and in 2010 with help from the UNDP, Tajikistan has created the Donor Anti-Corruption Forum which has sought to increase transparency in the distribution of foreign aid. Meanwhile, the conflict has strengthened the cross-border drug trade for all the countries that were part of the NATO's Northern Distribution Network. That situation led to an increase in the bribes demanded by border officials and other members of the transit sector. UNODC highlighted that approximately 90 MT of heroin was trafficked along the 'northern route' in 2010.

2. Deterrents and constraints

Implementing anti-corruption reforms required both an expansion *and* a specialisation of its institutional establishment. Specialised anti-corruption bodies have been set up in most of the FSU countries, usually under the direct supervision of the highest level of political authority (Armenia, Azerbaijan, Kazakhstan, Tajikistan, Russia and Ukraine). On the one hand that endows them with high prestige and shows the governments' 'political will'. For example, the Armenian Ethics Commission for High Ranking Officials was praised by the OECD. On the other hand it makes them susceptible to political influence. The Agency of the Republic of Kazakhstan on Fighting Economic and Corruption Crimes was accused of acting at the political whim of President Nazarbayev[11]; the Tajik Agency for State Financial Control and Fight against Corruption was created in 2008, but it is still understaffed and perceived as one of the country's most corrupt institutions[12]. In Ukraine, the National Anticorruption Committee has not held a meeting for over a year and the 800 million *hryvna* budget for implementing the anticorruption programme has never been allocated[13]. Such mixed results call into question the necessity for designated anti-corruption institutions at the national level.

A strong and effective law enforcement system is very much a necessary condition for modernisation (Della Porta and Vanucci 1999). Within the FSU countries, anti-corruption reforms related to law enforcement had two purposes: first to create a strong and reliable judicial system that could tackle corruption *outside* it, and second to eliminate corruption *within* the law enforcement agencies themselves.

Within the general anti-corruption framework, policies related to law enforcement agencies generally aim to increase the level of criminalization through *higher crime rates, higher sentences* and targeting of *high profile offenders*. The volume of *corruption –related crimes seem to have increased*. In Kazakhstan financial investigators identified nearly 1,800 corruption cases in public procurement between 2008 and 2012, with financial damage amounting to more than $46 million[14]. In 2012, the Russian authorities prosecuted 889 officials (including 244 city mayors and 114 lawmakers of various

in-tajikistan>

[11] (2012). *Kazakhstan Offers Rewards for Corruption Whistleblowers*, RFE/RL. Available at: <http://www.rferl.org/content/kazakhstan-rewards-offered-for-whistle-blowers/24697524.html>

[12] Idem note 10

[13] Khmara. Oleskii (2013). *Why is Ukraine incapable of fulfilling the demands of Fule's list? An analysis of state anticorruption policy.* Transparency International. Available at: <http://blog.transparency.org/2013/03/04/why-is-ukraine-incapable-of-fulfilling-the-demands-of-fules-list-an-analysis-of-state-anticorruption-policy/>

[14] (2013). *Коррупция в системе госзакупок нанесла государству ущерб на более чем 7 млрд тенге - финпол.* Zakon. Available at: <http://www.zakon.kz/4549532-korrupcija-v-sisteme-goszakupok-nanesla.html>

levels) and 1,159 law enforcement officials on corruption charges[15]. In Belarus, 276 corruption cases were prosecuted while the Ukrainian courts received 2,740 criminal cases involving corruption. In 2012, the damage from corrupt cases in Ukraine was nearly $225 million, according the Ukrainian Ministry of Justice. It is a challenge to interpret these statistics. On the one hand, they can be seen to show the efficiency of the justice system. On the other hand, they reveal that judicial resources have been directed towards anti-corruption, in accordance with the government priorities. That leads to the specialization of a significant body of police forces and magistrates in the anti-corruption area and puts additional pressure on the rest

Higher crime rates are associated with *harsher sentences*. The former Kyrgyz president Bakiyev and his son were sentenced to twenty five years in prison for abuse of office. In January 2013, David Kezerashvili, the former Georgian Defence Minister, was indicted for taking bribes and smuggling, facing a punishment of 11 to 15 years imprisonment[16].

The high profile of the offender is usually coupled with *significant financial prejudices*. In 2012, the region offered numerous examples of waves of high profile investigations, indictments and arrests. In Kazakhstan, Bergey Ryskaliev, the former mayor of Atyrau region, was accused of embezzling funds by awarding contracts for public procurement to his friends and relatives, signing contract agreements at wilfully inflated sums, and of making unjustified transfers of funds to contractors by fictitious acts of completion and subsequent withdrawals of the same funds through false accounts. The financial damage amounted to over $469,665,000[17]. The list includes mayors, ex ministers and MPs in Kyrgyzstan, ex-members of government in Armenia and Russia, and even a member of the President's family in Uzbekistan, all top officials fallen from grace or power. Therefore such arrests are interpreted in the countries mostly as acts of repression of adversaries. The politicised nature of anti-corruption reforms effectively undermined its core aim by *confusing the spheres of victim and offender*, as in the famous Ukraine Tymoshenko case. In Russia, in November 2012, President Putin dismissed the Defence Minister Anatoly E. Serdyukov after the police raided the property of a land agency involved in the sale on the open market of a valuable state-owned property near Moscow. It was known as the Oboronservis case and the losses to the Defence Ministry from corruption were allegedly $130 million[18]. Many had viewed Serdyukov as part of Putin's inner circle, and while the gesture might be seen as Putin's pledge in his third presidency to address corruption, it might just as well be the case that the Minister's active reforms of the armed forces by cutting costs and personnel were received with displeasure.

In order to reduce corruption within law enforcement agencies, a popular reform envisaged the use of *technology*. In Kyrgyzstan, a new recruitment system for judges

[15] Russian Legal Information Agency. (2013). *No 'untouchables' in fight against corruption – Kremlin.* RAPSI. Available at: <http://rapsinews.com/anticorruption_news/20130222/266500492.html>

[16] (2013). *Экс-министру обороны Грузии предъявлены обвинения в незаконном присвоении 12 миллионов долларов.* Available at: <http://www.apsny.ge/2013/soc/1359604728.php>

[17] (2013). Bnews.kz. Available at: <http://www.bnews.kz/ru/news/heading/glavnye_novosti/>

[18] RIA Novosti. (2013). Available at: *Naval Museum Director Arrested in $13 Million Fraud Case.* <http://en.rian.ru/military_news/20130413/180619780/Naval-Museum-Director-Arrested-in-13-Million-Fraud-Case.html>

put in place in 2012 consisted of computerised examinations. In Kazakhstan, President Nazarbayev initiated the "Law Enforcement Attestation Process", an exercise that involved competency testing for officers from a wide range of law enforcement agencies, but the exercise is also controversial.

New *repressive policies* have been associated with the desire to 'cleanse' the law enforcement agencies. Georgian President Saakashvili famously sacked the entire traffic police force to solve corruption. President Putin remarked that 'Georgia has a few thousand traffic cops; Russia has over a million. Firing them all at once is simply not an option[19].' Complementary policies involve *incentivizing* by increasing the salaries of the public sector and offering financial rewards to whistle-blowers. In November 2012 the Kyrgyz government announced a new scheme to reduce corruption among the judiciary by raising the salaries of judges. In August 2012, Kazakhstan allocated $213,000 a year to incentives for citizens to report cases of police corruption. Rewards may range from $300 to $1000 depending on the type of wrongdoing uncovered. The rewards are to be paid only in cases where officials are found guilty of corruption in court. It remains to be seen whether the policy will be successful.

Civil society, as a normative deterrent to corruption, is reportedly the weakest link in the former Soviet Union (Mungiu-Pippidi 2010), and is strongly associated with loose control of corruption (see **Figure 3**). Government pressures, restrictive regulatory frameworks, irregular funding and lack of support from state institutions are the main challenges faced by civil society in FSU countries.

Figure 3. Civil society and control of corruption

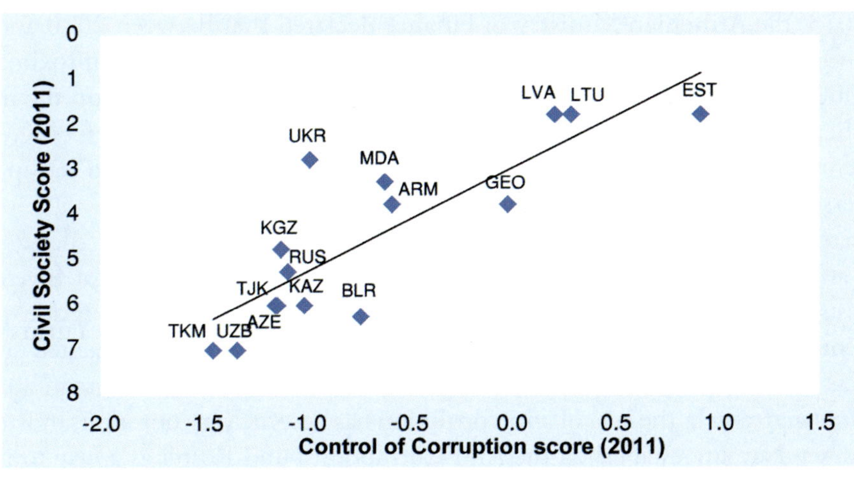

Data sources: Freedom House: Nations in Transit 2012
and Worldwide Governance Indicators, 2012

The low capability of civil society in constraining state capture is to be expected seeing the state of democracy in the region. Some countries, such as Belarus, are still categorized as 'repressive states' according to the 2013 Freedom House index of civil

---

[19] Aris, B. (2012). *Kremlin-Plans-New-Crackdown-on-Corruption-in-Russia*, -Telegraph. Available at:_<http:// www.telegraph.co.uk/sponsored/russianow/opinion/9253040/Russia-corruption-crackdown.html>

and political freedom rights. In Tajikistan, organizing an 'illegal gathering' can result in up to five years in prison, while in Kazakhstan participation in an 'illegal gathering' can lead to a $550 fine[20]. In both countries there are criminal penalties for insulting the President, and political dissident groups have been targeted. In 2012, Russia expanded the definition of 'treason', reintroduced defamation as a criminal offence and increased the fines associated with it to 2million roubles, or $61,000. Fines for individuals or organisations that violate the laws on arranging and participating in protests increased 150 and 300-fold respectively in June 2012[21]. New legislation now forces organisations that accept foreign funding or donations to register as 'foreign agents,' while also tightening membership criteria and increasing 'supervision.' and Court actions were initiated against important anticorruption NGOs such as GOLOS. NGOs in Russia have reported numerous cases of government intimidation such as police raids, the stationing of 'protective' units of police in offices and the expulsion of certain organisations, like USAID.

Due to the rising profile of civil society, some governments have started to create alliances with various NGOs. Such alliances can become iconic partnerships, but can also be the means by which politicians use an alternative voice to put forward their opinions – which is rather more commonly the case in the region under discussion here. Political interference can lead to preferential treatment, funding and corruption. In Uzbekistan, more than one NGO was involved in anti-corruption awareness campaigns; the 2012 Istanbul Action Plan report noticed that it was unclear "based on which criteria NGOs are selected to assist the Government in its anti-corruption efforts", while in Armenia, certain NGOs benefited from Government largesse. In April 2013, the Armenian Ministry of Finance declared that between 2010 and 2013 31 NGOs were funded from the state budget, together receiving approximately $ 1,215,000. Local media reported that no information could be found on the internet about the first three recipients of the funding. Furthermore, each of the six NGOs that had been sponsored without interruption over the three years had been set up by the same person, a certain Suren Nersisyan[22].

Nevertheless, successful cooperation between governments and civil society in the area of anti-corruption reforms is possible. In Armenia, the Association of Investigative Journalists (HETQ) was extensively involved in the 'Armenia against Corruption' project. The Central Election Commission of Ukraine requested and implemented a voter-awareness campaign with the OSCE during the parliamentary election there in 2012.

Online activism in the area of anti-corruption has become very notorious in Russia. In 2011 Alexey Navalny established the Anti-Corruption Fund Rospil as a way to increase transparency in public procurement. Rospil uncovered violations in the awarding of public contracts that amounted to 30 billion roubles in 2012. In November 2012 he launched a new project – RosZKH – which aimed to eradicate corrupt practices in housing and communal services. Similarly, in Ukraine, the site nashigroshi.org ("Our Money")

---

[20] Human Rights Watch. (2013). *World Report 2013 – Kazakhstan.* Available at: <http://www.hrw.org/world-report/2013/country-chapters/kazakhstan?page=2>

[21] ICNL. (2013). *NCO-Law-Monitor:-Russia.* Available at: <http://www.icnl.org/research/monitor/russia.html>

[22] (2013). *Harcum N 1160.* Available at: <http://www.givemeinfo.am/hy/case/1160/>

investigates corruption in the field of public contracts. Nashi Groshi has recently uncovered one $22,270 tender for snow removal from the courtyards of presidential administration buildings; another investigation showed that the annual travel expenses for members of the Supreme Administrative Court amounted to $270,685[23]. In Ukraine, online activists created an online civil map of corruption – Corrupt UA, where citizens can report corruption and place it on a map of the country.

The risks faced by civil society activists are very serious. After a recent criminal case Aleksey Navalny faces 10 years in prison for allegedly embezzling $500,000 from a state-controlled timber company in Kirov in 2009. Prosecutors initially dismissed the case, but federal officials revived it after Navalny became the most prominent leader of the street protests last year. In Belarus, the protests that followed the 2010 elections were brutally suppressed with hundreds of arrests. The government continued its policy of harassing civil activists and treated them as enemies of the state; draft amendments were signed by President Lukashenka to restrict funding options for civil society organisations[24]. In preparation for the upcoming elections in Azerbaijan, officials tend to prevent activists from taking part in any actions or protests[25].

The other factor inflicting normative constrains, a free media, is likewise doing rather badly in FSU. The 2013 World Press Freedom Index provided by Reporters Without Borders shows that media freedom is not high on the agenda of the FSU states. Captured media, violence against journalists and repressive governments are just a few of the characteristics of these countries. In Belarus, suppression of the media continued after the disputed elections in 2010; in 2011 95 journalists were detained during the summer's "silent protests"[26]. The Kazakhstan International Bureau of Human Rights reported that there were particular concerns regarding freedom of expression due to increases in libel suits against newspapers and journalists, along with physical attacks. In 2012, the two main opposition newspapers, Golos Respubliki and Vzglyad, were forced to halt publication a matter of days after the prosecutor-general's office announced that it had asked an Almaty court to ban a number of independent and opposition national news outlets, before any ruling had been made on the substance of the case[27]. In Ukraine, the 2012 Freedom House report noted an increasing monopolisation of national media by pro-government businessmen and politicians as well as an increase in paid political coverage. The same report remarked that in Uzbekistan, foreign broadcasting media outlets - Radio Free Europe/Radio Liberty, Voice of America, BBC World Service - cannot obtain permission to broadcast from within that country nor can they acquire accreditation for their offices. Furthermore, the authorities employ the practice of

---

[23] Khmara, O. (2013). *Public procurement websites fail to serve their purpose.* The Kyiv Post. Available at: <http://www.kyivpost.com/opinion/op-ed/public-procurement-websites-fail-to-serve-their-purpose-322563.html>

[24] Freedom House. (2012). *Nations in Transits - Belarus.* Available at: <http://www.freedomhouse.org/report/nations-transit/2012/belarus>

[25] (2013). *Азербайджан усиливает давление на НПО в преддверии выборов.* Available at: <http://panorama.am/ru/society/2013/03/22/guluzade/>

[26] Freedom House. (2012). *Nations in Transits - Belarus.* Available at: <http://www.freedomhouse.org/report/nations-transit/2012/belarus>

[27] Reporters Without Borders. (2012). *Opposition newspapers in Kazakhstan silenced ahead of court ruling.* Ifex. Available at: <http://www.ifex.org/kazakhstan/2012/12/07/opposition_newspapers_convicted/>

hiring "experts" to fashion criminal cases against journalists on charges ranging from national defamation to extremism.

3. Anticorruption and its prospects

The past decade was characterized by the globalisation of anti-corruption policies, conducted first and foremost through the multiplication of anti-corruption narratives, materialised in the form of international conventions. The conventions provided the international community with a standardised set of anti-corruption instruments. FSU countries have all become part of the global anti-corruption movement, at least formally. They have all ratified the United Nations Convention against Corruption (UNCAC) and Russia, Belarus, Moldova, Ukraine, Armenia, Georgia and Azerbaijan adopted the Council of Europe Civil and Criminal Law Conventions on Corruption, with Russia paving the way by signing the OECD Anti-Bribery Convention in April 2012.

The expansion of the anti-corruption domain was accompanied by the multiplication of international/regional partnerships that monitored and incentivised the implementation of anti-corruption reforms – the 'carrot and stick' approach, in fact.

- The OECD's Anti-Corruption Network for Eastern and Central Asia established the Istanbul Action Plan in 2003, a sub-regional peer review programme, for Ukraine, Armenia, Georgia, Azerbaijan, Kazakhstan, Kyrgyzstan, Tajikistan and Uzbekistan.
- The European Union has monitored anti-corruption reforms through the European Neighbourhood Policy and the Eastern Partnership. The latest report uncovered the lack of a coherent trend towards modernisation in the region. It expressed concerns regarding Azerbaijan in relation to the following areas: the electoral process, independence of the judiciary, protection of human rights, alignment of media freedom legislation to international standards, and the need to build a sustainable democracy. Praise went to Georgia, Moldova and to a certain extent Armenia, who were assured of continued financial support from Brussels.
- In the latest meeting of EURONEST (Baku, April 2012), Ukraine advanced its negotiations on the Association Agreement with the EU, making progress on the Visa Liberalisation Action Plans. The Agreement should be signed in November at the Vilnius Partnership Summit, if Ukraine steps up its anti-corruption efforts.
- Furthermore, within the Partnership for Modernisation, the EU has agreed to finance a joint anti-corruption project to be implemented by the Council of Europe and the Russian Business Ombudsman. The European Commission has made a priority of supporting projects aimed at promoting good governance in both Tajikistan and Kazakhstan.
- The World Bank chose Tajikistan as one of four European and Central Asian states in which to pilot its Governance and Anti-Corruption programme. The programme has worked to strengthen transparency and accountability in the public sector.
- National governments too have made available financial support in the region. The UK has a £42 million budget administered through the Department for International Development Central Asia programme.

Monitoring aspects that were considered particularly challenging in the area were high on the agenda of the international donors. USAID has allocated large amounts to the presidential and parliamentary elections in Armenia and Georgia $3.988.000 and $17 million respectively. However, it did not allocate any financial resources for the upcoming presidential elections in Azerbaijan, which will be held on the 16th of October 2013. The purpose of the funds was to ensure the transparency of the elections, to minimize corruption risks, and to assist electoral institutions and stakeholders in strengthening the political will to change the election culture. The idea is to enable the establishment of a competitive electoral environment as well as to support the broadcasting of TV programmes to increase citizens' awareness of their rights and duties as voters.

Since countries in this region are keen to attract foreign investment, the impact of corruption on the private sector is dealt with separately. The success of anti-corruption policies in the private sector is on the one hand related to making it a priority at the national level, and on the other hand to its being part of international economic agreements, conventions and institutions.

- Georgia, which is the most successful country in the region, has prioritised tackling anti-corruption in the private sector through the action plan of its 2010 – 2013 anti-corruption strategy.
- In Uzbekistan, President Karimov signed a new law entitled "On the defence of private property and the guarantee of the rights of owners", in September 2012. According to Karimov, the law was designed so that "every entrepreneur should know that he can without fear invest in his own business, expand production activities, increase production and generate income [...] keeping in mind that the government is guarding the legal rights of the property owner"[28].
- In order to secure property rights Kazakhstan ratified the Singapore Treaty on the Law of Trademarks and the Rome Convention for the Protection of Performers, Producers of Phonograms, and Broadcasting Organizations.
- Uzbekistan began the accession process to the CIS Free Trade Zone Agreement, while Armenia joined the World Trade Organization;
- Azerbaijan, Kazakhstan and Kirgizstan are part of the Extractive Industries Transparency Initiative (Tajikistan became a candidate in February 2013). In Kazakhstan, 123 extractive companies have chosen to implement the principles of the organization, which include reporting on all contracts and expenditure. Kazakh companies are 'close to compliant' with all EITI standards, but the Kazakh government should encourage all extractive companies to submit to audits which are of an international standard.
- In the FSU, the major barriers to business have been the licencing, customs and tax authorities. Recently, governments have started to address those problems in order to support economic development while reducing corruption. Russia eliminated the requirements for several preconstruction approvals and cadastral passports, Ukraine simplified the process of setting up a business and used an

---

[28] Cleek. A. (2013). *Uzbeksitan: New law promises no-fear investment climate.* Eurasianet.org. Available at: <http://www.eurasianet.org/node/65956>

effective time limit for processing transfer applications, Belarus simplified property transfers by eliminating the necessity to obtain municipality approval in Minsk; Kazakhstan introduced an electronic system for granting licences; Armenia, Georgia, Kyrgyzstan, Russia and Ukraine introduced one-stop-shops to simplify the procedures for obtaining approvals. Reduced taxation and the use of electronic forms in the tax system have proved successful policies in Ukraine, Russia and Georgia. However, Kyrgyzstan and Belarus have increased the costs of doing business by introducing additional taxes, policies somewhat related to anti-corruption concerns although they envisage wider and deeper change in society.

There are indeed a number of encouraging initiatives. In Russia, more than 20,000 firms formed coalitions to identify problematic legislation and to press for reform. One achievement was the simplification of obtaining permits, an accomplishment praised by the 2013 Doing Business Report. In Ukraine, a coalition of business associations demanded that the National Prosecutor launch an investigation into the mayor of Sumy's imposition of burdensome requirements on local businesses[29]. In Kyrgyzstan, the Bishkek Business Club has been working to introduce anti-corruption programmes for businesses. Furthermore, Kyrgyz business associations have offered to cooperate with the Council for Entrepreneurship Development, so that the new legislation is produced in cooperation. A group of young Russian entrepreneurs set up a creative anti-corruption initiative. They developed 'Bribr' which was an iPhone application (app.) to report bribes across Russia anonymously.

The countries from this region seem rather keen to implement reforms when the 'carrot' is access to markets, for example to labour markets in the case of Ukraine through the visa liberalisation programme, or protecting their own financial interests. The Cyprus crisis hit Russian business deposits hard, while the Magnistky Act put American investments under strain. For their part, the EU seems unwilling to upset its neighbours given its dependence on Russian gas and other regional natural resources.

In conclusion, the region does not show a coherent trend towards modernisation. Anti-corruption tools seem to have succeeded in Georgia, but failed dramatically in Turkmenistan. Countries such as Ukraine and Russia have fallen back after they had been making progress. Policy-wise, the most successful interventions have been those focused on changing the rules. However, these conclusions should be reassessed in the future because the countries in this region are at different stages in implementing these types of reforms.

References

Della Porta, D. &. Vannucci, A. (1999). *Corrupt Exchanges: Actors, Resources, and Mechanisms of Political Corruption* Aldine Transaction.

Galtung, F. (2005). Measuring the Immeasurable: Boundaries and Functions of (macro) Corruption Indices, in Galtung, F and Sampford, C. (eds.), *Measuring Corruption*. Burlington: Ashgate, 101-132

---

[29] Centre for International Private Enterprise. (2011). *Annual Report.* Available at: <http://cipe.org/sites/default/files/publication-docs/AR2011_final_PDF.pdf>

Haller, D., Shore C. (Eds.) (2005). *Corruption: Anthropological Perspectives*, Pluto Press.

Klitgaard, R. (1988). *Controlling Corruption*, University of Berkeley, CA: University Press.

Knack, S. (2006). Measuring corruption in Eastern Europe and Central Asia: a critique of cross-country Indicators', *World Bank Policy Research Working Paper*: 3968. <http://www.wds.worldbank.org/servlet/WDSContentServer/WDSP/IB/2006/07/13/000016406_200 60713140304/Rendered/PDF/wps3968.pdf>

Krastev, I. (2004), *Shifting Obsessions: Three Essays on the Politics of Anticorruption*, Budapest: Central European University Press.

Ledeneva, A. (2003). The Commonwealth of Independent States Regional Corruption Report' in Hodess. R, Inowlocki, T. and Walfe. T. (Eds.) *Transparency International Global Corruption Report, 2003*, Profile Books, 165-176 (see <www.transparency.org>).

Ledeneva, A. (2006), *How Russia Really Works*. Cornell University Press

Mungiu-Pippidi, A. (2010). The other transition. *Journal of Democracy*, *21*(1), 120-127.

Mungiu-Pippdi (2013). *The Good, the Bad, the Ugly: Controlling Corruption in the European Union, Working Paper no. 35, Berlin: European Research Centre for Anticorruption and State-Building, accessible at* <http://www.againstcorruption.eu/reports/the-good-the-bad-and-the-ugly-controlling-corruption-in-the-european-union/>

Persson, A., Rothstein, B. and Teorell, J. (2010) 'The Failure of Anti-corruption Policies: A Theoretical Mischaracterization of the Problem', QoG Working Paper

5. Top of the Class. The Case of Estonia

AARE KASEMETS

Estonia is internationally perceived as the post-communist positive outlier, which has made perhaps the most spectacular progress in the world, from a totalitarian Soviet Union regime to a stable parliamentary democracy in less than twenty years. Since 2000 Estonia is ranked by World Bank in the group of democratic countries with open access governance regime, but few social science studies exist which offer explantions of her success. This report offers an agency based explanation of Estonia's success story, considering that anticommunist political elites, which have managed to stay continuously in government since the fall of USSR have played the largest role in building control of corruption.

Introduction

The development of Estonian, also Latvian and Lithuanian societies after the restoration of their independence in 1991 can be divided into three transition periods (Lauristin and Peeter Vihalemmm, 2009). *The first period* is the creation of the new constitutional and social order and carrying out basic economic reforms in order to escape the deep crisis that followed the collapse of the socialist planned economy. In Estonia, where radical liberal economic reforms were carried out and a suitable environment was created for the development of a market economy within four years, the first stage was the shortest of all three Baltic countries. As the country was internationally praised for its successful market reforms, the weakening of social security was to some extent compensated by general optimism regarding the country's economic and technological development. *The second period* of the transition ranges from the start of accession talks with the European Union. Estonia was invited to join the EU as early as 1997. All three Baltic States received an official invitation to join the EU in 1999. The prospect of joining the EU as well as the opportunity to achieve NATO membership formed the solid basis for political consensus that was necessary for implementing the political and economic reforms (e.g. initiation of the first anti-corruption strategy "Honest State" 2003-2007). *The third period* began with the accession to the EU on 1 May 2004. This period is characterized by a general increase in individual prosperity, followed by a deep economic downturn. The beginning of the period saw strong economic growth in all Baltic States: the countries experienced a GDP growth of 10% and more from the spring of 2005 to the autumn of 2007. The overheating of the economy was not taken as a serious threat; most of people enjoyed the feeling of relaxation after the hard years of struggling with poverty. The hard economic crisis of 2008-2009 was answered adequately and soon growth resumed. The cost of the recovery included severe cuts in public finances/services, shrinking family budgets and a wave of emigration among the skilled labour (See Lauristin & Vihalemm 2011). Finally, a *fourth period* can be added to Lauristin and Vihalemm' periodization, which started after the deep economic recession and included the joining to OECD in the end of 2010 (Larustin 2013; OECD Better Life Index 2013).

According to *the WGI Control of Corruption* score (see **Table 1**) Estonia has been a "green country" since 2000, although a surge in corruption scandals scandals was experienced after the latest elections. *Freedom in the World* and *Polity IV* both confirm, that Estonia has achieved in 1992-2011 the highest level of democracy – the scores are near the maximum. According to *the Nations in Transit* scores Estonia estimated in the range of 80-85% of the maximum value of the index, but it also means a very good result among transition countries. *The Economist*'s assessment of Estonia's democracy 2006-2011 has remained at a somewhat lower level (75-80% of the maximum value). This result (in 2011 34th of 167) places Estonia into category of incomplete democracies, mostly due to political participation subindex (Mölder & Pettai 2013). In *the Heritage Economic Freedom Index* 2012 Estonia is 16th of 197, in *the Press Freedom Index* 2011/2012 3rd of 179, in 2013 11th.[1]

Table 1. Control of corruption over succes global cases

Country	Region	Control of Corruption score			Control of Corruption % rank			Rank in the region (2009)
		2009	1998	Change	2009	1998	Change	
Uruguay	Latin America	1.22	0.87	0.35	86	80	6	2 (20)
Estonia	Eastern Europe and post-Soviet Union	1.00	0.60	0.40	80	71	9	2 (28) after Slovenia
South Korea	East Asia	0.52	0.27	0.25	71	65	6	3 (6)
Ghana	Sub-Saharan Africa	0.06	-0.25	0.31	60	48	12	9 (48)

Source: Worldwide Governance Indicators, World Bank; Mungiu-Pippidi et al. (2011). Excerpt.

Estonia may not be entirely free of corruption, but foundations of ethical universalism in governance seem to have taken root (Mungiu-Pippidi et al. 2011). The latest sociological follow-up survey carried out by the Ministry of Justice (2010) confirmed the positive trend in anti-corruption attitudes in general and found also that there are quite remarkable differences between different target groups (residents, entrepreneurs, public sector) and socio-demographic divisions (gender, nationality, age, region, etc.).[2] For instance, the attitude towards giving "presents" has changed and it can be assumed

---

[1] 2012 Index of Economic Freedom <www.heritage.org>; Reporters Without Borders 2012-2013 <en.rsf.org> [09.06.2013]

[2] Estonian Ministry of Justice (2010). "Corruption in Estonia: the study of three target groups 2010", Criminal policy studies 13, Tallinn

that the tradition of giving presents, typical to post-Soviet countries, is slowly vanishing from Estonia. 54% of residents consider it corruption if an official accepts a present in return for his or her services. This is 10 percentage points more than in 2006. The number of entrepreneurs considering accepting of presents to be corruption has increased as well to 62% presently, whereas it was 57% earlier.

1. The foundations of corruption control

One of few attempts to explain Estonia's success is the control of corruption equilibrium model - developed by Alina Mungiu-Pippidi et al. (2011). She argues that Estonia has registered improvement in all essential four dimensions of control of corruption and leaves open the question on why has this country registered better progress that its Baltic neighbours, which she answers in part by modernization theory (Estonia was already more urban and literate that its neighbours end 19th century). A match of data on Estonian institutional transition with the integrated elements of control of corruption equilibrium model matrix shows that most of elements are presently in place. During the first government of Mart Laar (1992-1995), policies have already been implemented that reduced material resources and strengthened legal constraints. Estonia pioneered important liberal reforms, for instance the adoption of a flat tax, which then became very trendy in Eastern Europe as a tool against tax evasion and informal economy, and embraced very advanced e-government reforms inspired from neighbouring Finland. Since February 2000, when the Estonian Parliament passed legislation guaranteeing Internet access to the general population, Estonia has become one of the most technologically connected populations in Europe, and some have nicknamed the country 'E-stonia'. In addition to high rates of Internet usage, nearly 90% of the population subscribes to mobile telephone service, and more than half have digital identity cards. The country's high rates of Internet usage come not only from the high numbers of household computers, but also from a strong commitment to free Internet access points across the country. All schools in Estonia are connected to the Internet, more than half of all households pay their bills electronically, and the state portal <www.eesti.ee> allows citizens to access their various official records, logging into other information systems (for example e-Tax Board or the Land Registry, fill in requests or pay bills (Kasemets & Leps 2010). According to recent Estonia's Action Plan for Participation in Open Government Partnership (OGP, 2012)[3] "The transparency of governance, the fight against corruption and the engagement of citizens in public governance play the central role in the OGP... Estonia has abided by the principles of openness and transparency by creating the respective legal framework and extensively using modern technological solutions in public administration". Since 2007 the Estonian company registration and management portal allows one to establish a company, to change the registered information of an existing company and to submit annual reports online (24h e-service in Estonian and English). In March 2013, Estonian e-Annual Reporting was honoured as decade's best e-Government content during the United Nations World Summit at the Information Society +10 event

---

[3] Open Government Partnership, "Country Commitments", <www.opengovpartnership.org/countries> [02.12.2012]

at UNESCO headquarters in Paris.[4] Another cornerstone of control of corruption is the system of public e-procurement.[5] Especially on the level of local authorities there have been many criminal proceedings and juridical borderline cases. Since 2013 a new cloud-based information application <www.riigipilv.ee> is making the financial data of Estonian local authorities public for everyone who would like to view, download, compare and analyse the budget data.[6] These kind of e-Governance tools are supporting the conditions of the social control of corruption and more transparent decision-making.

In brief, Estonia is characterized by a very high availability of public information and outstanding technological level. Estonia ranks first in the world in terms of Internet freedom (see **Table 2**) and on the other hand the use of public information with a high level of legislative guarantees of public access to information is a good basis for government transparency and combating corruption.

Table 2. Central government information in the public records
(Disclosure index based on OECD data 2011)

Top 5	State budget	Annual activity reports of the ministries and offices	Audits	Explanatory memoranda of policy documents / draft acts	Business contracts (e.g. public procurement data)	Names and salary of civil servants	Administrative databases of ministries and offices	Content, procedures and rules of data collection	Internal procedures and guidelines of authorities	State authorities structures and functions	Annual Information Freedom Report	Guidance on information freedom process/ rights	Disclosure index (max 24p)*
Estonia	2	2	2	2	2	2	2	2	2	2	2	2	24
Hungary	2	2	2	2	2	-	2	2	2	2	2	2	22
S-Korea	2	2	2	2	2	-	2	2	2	2	2	2	22
Slovenia	2	2	2	2	-	-	2	2	2	2	2	2	20
Finland	2	2	2	2	2	-	2	2	1	1	-	2	18

Source: OECD Factbook 2011, calculations by Peeter Vihalemm (2013: 74-75). *Calculations: the law requires - 2 points; according to administrative decisions traditionally published - 1 point.

Legal and normative constraints also work. Estonia had the most radical policy towards the Soviet era judiciary, replacing most of it and starting practically over with new magistrates trained within a few months. Normative constraints are also high, with a public opinion intolerant of bribing, though relatively tolerant towards other forms of particularism, an active civil society, and a free press which benefited from investment from its Scandinavian neighbours. Civil society and government agreed to dedicate a part of European funds to civil society activities, and signed a pact including commitments on the rule of law by both parties (Kasemets & Leps 2010).

---

[4] Centre of Registers and Information Systems 'e-Estonia strikes again' <http://www.rik.ee/en/news/e-estonia-strikes-again> [10/6/2013]

[5] RISO (2012) State information system, e-Procurement, <www.riso.ee/en/node/102> [02.12.2012]

[6] ERR News (2012) *New System Puts Local Government Spending Under Virtual Microscope*. Published: 21.09.2012. Available from: <http://news.err.ee/Sci-Tech/7ee96ac8-05b8-43c9-b60b-38eb0cffc2dd> [25.11.2012]

Media outlets are numerous, and legal protections for press freedom exist and are practiced. Also, there is little regulation over the establishment and functioning of media outlets, and investigative reporters are protected from victimization by powerful state or NGO actors in other countries. Considering the small size of the country, the Estonian public enjoys an impressively diverse selection of print and electronic sources of information representing a range of political viewpoints. Most of these media outlets are privately owned (e.g. Scandinavian firms, 'free from local political pressure'). *Freedom House* (2012) assessed that: "The mainstream press in Estonia continued to be free and robust, although its economic situation - in an era of multiple media and information sources, and in a small national market - was always somewhat fragile." In The Freedom House *Freedom of the Press Index 2012* rankings Estonia was 22th of 197 (next countries in CEE region: Czech Republic 25th, Slovakia 31st, Lithuania 40th, Poland and Slovenia both 47th). In *Reporters Without Borders Index* 2012 raitings Estonia was 3rd of 179 (after Norway and Finland) and in 2013 11th.[7] In addition, Estonian society excels in a very large and active free media information consumption. The overall level of media use is significantly above the EU average (9th of 27).[8] Estonia has very liberal media environment and high availability of public information. Freedom of the media (e.g. Internet freedom) and the use of information is a good basis for *combating corruption (see* **Table 2***).*

2. Domestic agency as main explanation

Nationalism and liberalism combine to explain Estonia's pots 1989 success, but personalities also matter and strong leadership is essential in anti-corruption policy design and implementation of regulatory governance reforms. This is the case of Prime Ministers Mart Laar (1992-1995; 1999-2002) and also Juhan Parts (2003-2005). As John Tierney, NYT, reported in his retrospective column (2006): "[Estonia] transformed itself from an isolated, impoverished part of the Soviet Union thanks to a former prime minister, Mart Laar, a history teacher who took office not long after Estonia was liberated. He was 32 years old and had read just one book on economics: "Free to Choose," by Milton Friedman, which he liked especially because he knew Friedman was despised by the Soviets. Laar was politically naïve enough to put the theories into practice."[9] The centre-right has basically won every single general election with the exception of one in 1995 (mixed coalition 1995-99). During Parts's government, also political financing regulation became stricter and a first national anti-corruption strategy "Honest State" was adopted.

Other responsible politicians have been active, for instance MPs, who contributed in 1990ies. For example, the Code of Ethics for Civil Servants was adopted as an Appendix of the Civil Service Act in 1999. Behind this Act and Code of Ethics were two MPs, who had western academic background – Mr Ivar Tallo, now Director of Estonian e-Governance Academy (Social Democratic Party) and Mr Daimar Liiv, now Judge (Reform Party). This kind of cooperation between politicians belonging to different political

---

[7] 2012 Index of Economic Freedom <www.heritage.org>; Reporters Without Borders 2012-2013 <en.rsf.org> [09.06.2013]

[8] Eurostat (2011). Media use in the European Union. Standard Eurobarometer 76, Autumn 2011 <http://ec.europa.eu/public_opinion/index_en.htm>

[9] Tierney, J. (2006) "New Europe's Boomtown", NYT, <www.nytimes.com/2006/09/05/opinion/05tierney.html?_r=1> [12.06.2013]

parties was quite usual in Estonian Parliament in 1990ies.[10] Secondly, another important fact is that many political leaders, active in policy- and law-making in 1990ies, had also been active in the independence movement 1985 to 1991. A review of the electoral campaigns of political parties 1992 to 2011, anti-corruption as a campaign platform was most visible in 1992 (Mart Laar *et al.*) and 2003 (Juhan Parts & *Team of Incorruptibles*). After Gorbatshov's *perestroika* and Estonian "singing revolution" 1987–1991 it was quite common to think that corruption and other unethical phenomenon are directly related to the Soviet political regime. In 1992, the main political slogan of Mart Laar' *ProPatria Party* for the general elections was "Clean the political power!" ("Plats puhtaks!"). Ten years later, the same kind of new slogan "Incorruptible!" ("Äraostmatud") was also successfully used by *ResPublica Party* for general elections on 2003. But not all were equally incorruptible. As Freedom House (2012) reported: "Influence peddling became a major issue in December 2011, when it was revealed that three prominent right-wing politicians (including two MPs) had been operating a private business that helped Russian citizens obtain residency permits in Estonia through sometimes questionable investment schemes."[11] The case of Reform Party donations scandal confirms once again that preventing political corruption is a struggle which cannot be relaxed.'[12]

Estonia's control of corruption benefitted from a favourable international context (NATO and EU accession), but it was mostly domestically driven by political elites supported by the Estonian society. Civil society, media and public administration have all gradually matured. Many provisions of Anti-Corruption Act, Political Parties Act and Public Service Act adopted until 2012 will come into force in 2013 and in 2014. In the same time new proposals are under discussion. In other words, the construction is not over yet.

References

Lauristin, M. & Vihalemm, P. (2009). The political agenda during different periods of Estonian transformation: External and internal factors - *Journal of Baltic Studies,* 40, 1, pp. 1–28

Lauristin, M. & Vihalemm, P. (2011). Satisfaction with outcomes of Baltic transition in spring 2011 - in Lauristin, M. (ed.) Estonian Human Development Report (Baltic Issue), pp. 10-12, 18-20

Lauristin, M. (2013). Introduction – in Heidmets, M. (ed.) Estonia in the world. Estonian Human Development Report 2012/2013, p. 55

Mungiu-Pippidi, A. et al. (2011). *Contextual Choices in Fighting Corruption: Lessons Learned* (NORAD, Report 4/2011), p xiii. Available from: <www.norad.no/en/tools-and-publications/publications/publication?key=383808> [10.06.2013]

Mölder, M. & Pettai, V. (2013). Vabadus ja demokraatia (Freedom and democracy) – in Heidmets, M. (ed.) Estonia in the world. Estonian Human Development Report 2012/2013, pp. 61-64 <http://www.kogu.ee/wp-content/uploads/2013/05/EIA20122013.pdf> (in Estonian)

Vihalemm, P. (2013) Infokeskond ja meediavabadus (Information environment and media freedom) - In Heidmets, M. (ed.) Estonia in the World. Estonian Human Development Report 2012/2013 (in Estonian), pp. 70-73

---

[10] Based on this Code of Ethics for Civil Servants, all state agencies, including the Chancellery of the *Riigikogu*, had to develop their own regulations and training programmes. The author led the working group of Code of Ethics for Parliamentary Civil Service, 1999-2000.

[11] Freedom House (2012), <www.freedomhouse.org/report/nations-transit/2012/estonia> [08.06.2013]

[12] Saar, J. (2012). Political corruption: the rule, bad taste or an offense? Postimees, (in Estonian): <http://arvamus.postimees.ee/854392/poliitiline-korruptsioon-tavanorm-maitsevaaratus-voi-suutegu/> [26.05.2012]

6. Hidden Depths. The Case of Hungary[1]

MIHÁLY FAZEKAS, LAWRENCE PETER KING
AND ISTVÁN JÁNOS TÓTH

This report investigates corruption risk of EU funds spending in Hungary within the framework of the Public Procurement Law. Its finding is that in spite of what is a tight regulatory framework EU funds are likely to fuel the abuse of public spending. Even though public procurement using EU funds faces considerably more stringent regulation, their use poses much greater corruption risks when compared with funds procured domestically and corruption risks are particularly pronounced for large projects. The report also argues that large-scale institutionalized corruption in Hungary may be widespread and driven primarily by political cycles. Such corruption, often labelled "legal corruption", typically involves neither bribery nor collusion between lower level bureaucrats and private individuals; rather, it operates through contractual relationships which benefit the highest echelons of the political and business elite. There are a small number of new anti-corruption initiatives of the new government which entered office in 2010, but while they might indicate a positive step towards higher public sector integrity, their results are yet to be seen.

Introduction

Hungary scores as one of Central and Eastern Europe's most corrupt countries according to the widely used but hotly contested Worldwide Governance Indicators[2] (see chapter 3 of this book) as well as when measured in the Quality of Goverment EU Regional Data survey (see chapter 8 of this book). Research looking at Hungarian corruption in more detail using qualitative methods or media content analysis reveals a great deal of additional evidence relating to the phenomenon's structure and its evolution over time.

Taking the available information together, Hungary appears to be a borderline case between limited and open access orders with considerable movements or swings between these ideal types (Mungiu-Pippidi et al. 2011). There are islands of excellence in the state which exercise a great deal of autonomy from potential societal captor agents; however, those institutions are regularly contested as for example in the recurrent attacks on the Hungarian National Bank in the last decade or so.

---

[1] The research was made possible by support from two EU funded projects at the Corvinus University of Budapest (TAMOP 4.2.2.B and ANTICORRP: Grant agreement no: 290529) and the authors' voluntary contributions.
[2] For a more detailed discussion of criticism see: Kaufmann, Kraay, & Mastruzzi, 2007; Kurtz & Schrank, 2007a, 2007b

Even though the exact path of evolution is yet to be fully documented, there is considerable evidence pointing to the increased institutionalisation of corruption in Hungary (**Figure 1**). Networks of private and public actors appear to have evolved for pursuing particularistic goals using public resources (Jancsics & Jávor, 2012; Szántó, Tóth, & Varga, 2012; Szántó & Tóth, 2008). A clear sign of increased institutionalisation is the emergence of the role of the 'broker' who sells an understanding of corrupt transactions and knowledge of actors in a wide range of sectors and institutional contexts.

Figure 1. Ratio of occurrence of multiplayer, chain-like corruption cases
in the Hungarian media, 2001-2009, % (548 cases of suspected corruption).

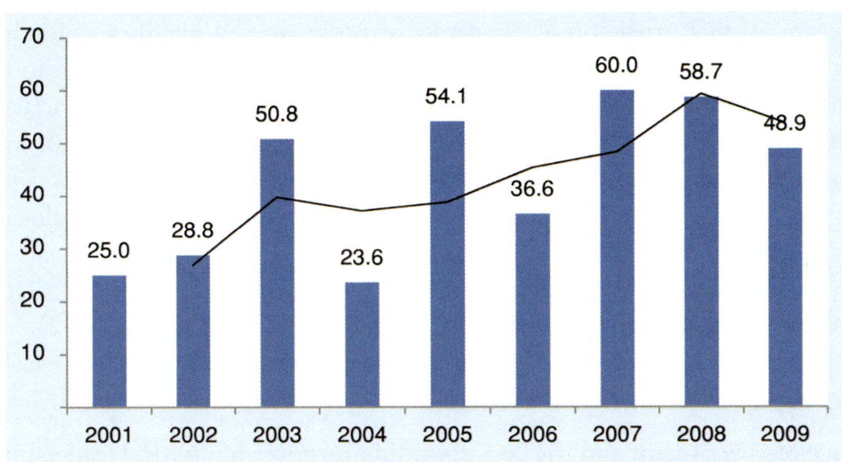

Source: Szántó et al., 2012 p. 148.

Based on court proceedings and interview evidence, it seems that corrupt networks have reached the highest echelons of the political and business elite, and they have contributed to political election campaigns as well as benefiting individual members. Corruption has become a top priority and a frequently quoted objective in election campaigns, and corruption scandals which hit the previous government most probably contributed to the landslide victory of Fidesz in 2010.

EU funds have become the single most important source of public investment in Hungary and by now they play a major role in overall public spending. Their disbursement is certainly affected by the competing principles of particularism and universalism so strikingly present in the functioning of the Hungarian state. In order to explore further the dynamics and evolution of the governance regime of Hungary this chapter delivers preliminary **evidence on large-scale institutionalized corruption[3] in EU funds spending in Hungarian public procurement based on data from 2009-2012.** We looked only at EU funding which is spent by Hungarian public and semi-public organisations (i.e. mixed public-private owned) through public procurement regulated by the Public Procurement Law. Hence, our study almost entirely covers the Cohesion Fund and much of the Structural Funds spending, but not the Common Agricultural Policy funds.

---

[3] For a detailed discussion of large-scale or legal corruption see: Kaufmann & Vincente, 2011

Our findings come from the analysis of interviews with key individuals who have witnessed corrupt transactions and from a large database recording every public procurement procedure in Hungary which was conducted under national or EU public procurement law between 1ˢᵗ of January 2009 and 31ˢᵗ of December 2012. This database contains over 56,000 contract awards, allowing for an unprecedentedly detailed view of public spending and high-level corruption.

This analysis of a borderline governance regime occurs at the onset of a new anticorruption campaign. The Fidesz government has launched a range of policies aimed at curbing corruption in the public sector, integrated into the Corruption Prevention Program of the Public Administration launched in early 2012 (for full list of recent initiatives check the online version of this Article on www.againstcorruption.eu). While these initiatives may represent a positive step towards greater public sector integrity, results are yet to be seen. Our analysis can explore only the baseline before any of the policies could actually take serious effect, but future research employing similar methodology will be able look into changes potentially attributable to the new initiatives.

Hungary is one of the top beneficiaries of EU cohesion policies with allocated per capita spending close to 3,000 EUR for 2007-2013. However, EU funds absorption has been an issue with contracted ratio of 64% by the end of 2011 falling slightly below the Central and Eastern Europe (CEE) average of 67% (KPMG, 2012).

1. Government favouritism evidence

Change of government and the corresponding turnover of political leadership seems to drastically alter the winning chances of companies in the public procurement market, both EU- and non-EU funded. In interviews, top managers of large construction, IT, and health care companies supplying public organisations all supported the view that the swings in market shares of companies reflect the changing preferences of the political leadership for particular well-connected companies. According to this interpretation, success in the public procurement market depends much more on political connections than on the competitiveness of companies, implying a predominantly particularistic allocation of public resources. Such corruption, often described as "legal corruption", typically does not involve bribery nor collusion between lower level bureaucrats and private individuals; rather, it operates through contractual relationships benefiting the highest echelons of the political and business elite (Kaufmann & Vicente, 2005).

Such claims are demonstrated by tracking the changes in market shares of the largest companies before and after the new government entered office (**Figure 2**), but they are also underpinned by regression analysis looking at the whole public procurement market financed from EU funds (Annex 1). **Figure 2** amply demonstrates that the companies with the largest market share throughout the one and a half years leading up to the elections in the first half of 2010 lost about 25-30% of their combined market share. This change was accompanied by a comparable increase in the total market share of companies dominating the post-election market between the second half of 2011 and 2012 (the one year period between 2010H2 and 2011H1 was excluded as it was a transitory period between the two governments).

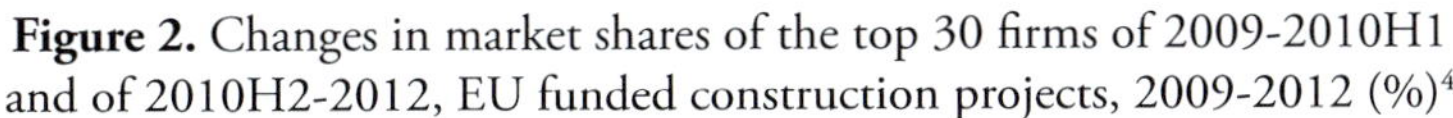

Figure 2. Changes in market shares of the top 30 firms of 2009-2010H1 and of 2010H2-2012, EU funded construction projects, 2009-2012 (%)[4]

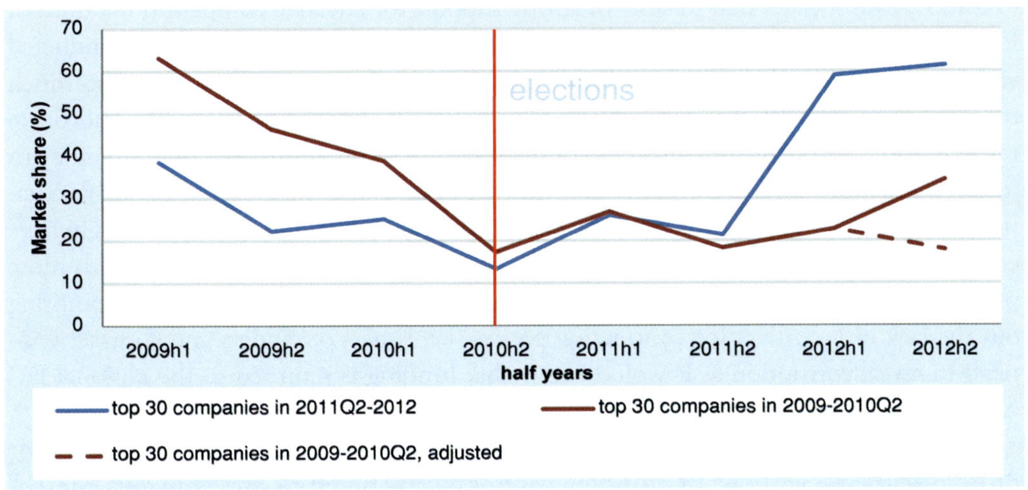

Source: MaKAB

Note: market share of company i in time t=total value of contracts won by company i in EU funded construction in time t / total value of contracts won in EU funded construction in time t

One of our previous reports found similar patterns throughout the public procurement market, albeit the magnitude of seemingly politically driven spending is comparatively greater for EU-funded contracts (Fazekas & Tóth, 2013). Regression analysis in Annex 1 supports the same conclusions while looking at the entire EU-funded public procurement market and taking into account the effects of companies' main market size, company size, amount of prior capital investment, location of headquarters, and profit margin.

Thus, based on the available evidence, it is likely that at least 25-30% of EU-funded construction spending is driven directly by politics in Hungary, but it is conceivable that the proportion is as high as 80-90%, for several interviewees suggested that contracts going to the opposite political camp's companies function as "payment" for future contracts for companies whose political connections currently hold the power, but might lose it in the future. Evidence to date indicates that large-scale institutionalized corruption is widespread in Hungary.

2. EU funds spending compared to national public procurement

When comparing public procurement contracts financed from EU funds to those without any EU sources on some elementary corruption risk indicators[5], EU funds perform considerably worse than national funds. This underpins the claim that EU funds fuel the abuse of public spending in spite of a tight regulatory framework.

---

[4] It is possible to adjust the combined market share of the top 30 companies of 2009-2010H1 in 2012H2 because the figure is highly upwards-distorted by a single highway construction contract. In addition, interview evidence points to strong political involvement in the management of that contract award procedure.

[5] For a full discussion of these and further indicators see: Fazekas, Tóth, & King, 2012

33.8% of contracts awarded for projects financed by EU funds throughout 2009-2012 received only one bid as opposed to 29% of contracts financed from purely national funds (**Table 1**). This implies that in spite of strong support for effective competition, a third of EU funds spending by Hungarian authorities through public procurement is conducted with no competition whatsoever. Modifying contracts after contract award is also much more frequent with EU-funded projects than nationally funded ones (17.7% and 6.5% respectively), a surprising difference as contract modifications are allowed only in a few unforeseen situations such as extremely bad weather or unusually high exchange rate fluctuations. As contract modifications allow for pushing the prices up and quality down after the competitive contract award process ends, we may suspect that EU funds are much more prone to corrupt rent extraction. Interview evidence supports this interpretation, pointing out the lack of incentives for contracting parties (i.e. issuers of tenders and contract winners) to reveal corruption as it would imply that funding is returned to the national EU funding disbursement agency, i.e. loss of external funding for both parties.

Regression results underline that such differences between contracts awarded for projects with and without EU funding cannot be attributed to some obvious alternative explanation such as contract size, market of spending, or type of issuer (Results of regressions on the differences between EU funded and nationally financed public procurement contracts are available in the online version of this Article on www.againstcorruption.eu).

Table 1. Selected corruption risk indicators of public procurement contract awards with and without EU funds (2009-2012)

Period	2009		2010		2011		2012		Total 2009-2012	
Proportion of occurrence among contracts with/without EU funds	Public procurement contracts using EU funds?		Public procurement contracts using EU funds?		Public procurement contracts using EU funds?		Public procurement contracts using EU funds?		**Public procurement contracts using EU funds?**	
	NO	YES	NO	YES	NO	YES	NO	YES	NO	YES
single bidder	30.9%	40.2%	30.6%	43.4%	25.7%	28.0%	28.1%	24.9%	**29.0%**	**33.8%**
non-open procedure	43.5%	39.7%	32.9%	32.2%	36.9%	36.6%	45.4%	56.9%	**39.2%**	**40.9%**
no call for tenders in Official Journal	48.7%	38.9%	25.4%	23.8%	56.2%	66.5%	55.2%	73.5%	**44.7%**	**50.9%**
accelerated submission deadline (<21 days)	17.7%	20.8%	26.5%	28.4%	24.0%	40.7%	19.9%	26.4%	**23.2%**	**29.2%**
extremely short submission deadline (<12 days)	2.7%	3.1%	2.3%	1.9%	2.3%	3.5%	2.6%	3.4%	**2.4%**	**2.6%**
contract modification	4.6%	16.2%	9.8%	25.4%	8.0%	22.0%	2.5%	4.6%	**6.5%**	**17.7%**
assessment criteria contains non-price elements	47.2%	52.0%	48.4%	64.3%	35.8%	40.4%	34.0%	34.1%	**41.8%**	**48.0%**
Total N	7,711	3,144	11,019	6,467	8,148	5,904	8,514	5,340	35,392	20,855

Source: MaKAB
Note: differences deemed substantive are highlighted in grey.

The most striking characteristic of these corruption risk indicators, called 'irregularities' by the European Court of Auditors (European Court of Auditors, 2012), is that they are not irregular nor are they random. They are particularly high for those companies whose market share appears to be driven by the political cycle as identified in the previous section and in Annex 1. This can be interpreted as meaning that those companies which win public procurement contracts funded by the EU with the help of their political connections tend to win under conditions prone to corruption. The point is well demonstrated in the differences among companies which perform according to what a standard economic logic would predict and those which considerably under- or over-perform compared to a pure economic model[6] (**Table 2**).

For example, companies under- or over-performing are 2 to 3 times more likely to experience contract modification after their contract has been approved than those which perform according to a standard economic logic. But differences are similarly striking in the frequency of accelerated and extremely short submission deadlines.

Table 2. Selected corruption risk indicators according to company groups,
EU funded public procurement, 2011

	single bidder	non-open procedure	no call for tenders in Official Journal	accelerated submission deadline (<21 days)	extremely short submission deadline (<12 days)	contract modification	assessment criteria contains non-price elements
under-performers	24.6%	37.1%	58.5%	42.0%	6.4%	33.5%	49.3%
in line with econ. predictions	22.9%	28.2%	45.0%	36.2%	0.4%	11.4%	39.2%
over-performers	27.3%	34.3%	52.2%	41.1%	2.7%	23.7%	48.0%

Source: MaKAB
Note: N=266

All this evidence underpins the hypothesis that EU funds represent much higher corruption risks than spending of Hungarian funds in spite of considerably more stringent regulation. As corruption risks are particularly pronounced for large projects and for companies dependent on their political connections for winning contracts, EU funds-related corruption is most probably driven by national politics. Our findings are confirmed by data from the previous and the current governments; that is the whole period of 2009-2012, pointing to the potentially systemic nature of corruption in post-communist Hungary.

---

[6] Under-performance is defined as large negative error in the regression of Annex 1 taking into account standard economic variables determining market performance, while over-performance is large positive error in the same regressions. Those companies which have regression error close to zero are deemed as performing according to what is expected.

Recommendations

In order for the EU and Hungary to combat corruption in EU funds spending and to avoid waste of public resources they might consider the following:

- *Ensure effective transparency and active access to information on public procurement*

Timely information provision in a format readily comprehensible and at a location easily accessible is the only way to fight corruption; in other words through transparency. Information which is outdated, barely comprehensible to non-experts, and accessible only after a large investment of time and effort helps fighting corruption little more than no transparency at all.

- *Close loopholes in public procurement regulation.*

Exceptions, emergency regulations, and minimum thresholds are abused far too often. By closing those routes and ensuring a minimum level of transparency for the currently loosely regulated purchases would make hiding corruption much more difficult.

- *Review the quality of outcomes and prices of inputs rather than the procedures of spending.*

The current administrative framework focuses largely on procedural and financial compliance, which makes the administration of EU funded projects costly while achieving little in preventing corruption. Refocusing audits or reviews on the quality of outcomes and the price of inputs might work better in revealing and so curbing corruption.

References

European Court of Auditors. (2012). *Annual Report on the Implementation of the Budget concerning financial year 2011*. Brussels.

Fazekas, M., & Tóth, I. J. (2013). *Political Influence in the Public Procurement Market? Analysis of market share 2009-2011 – preliminary results*. Corruption Research Centre, Budapest.

Fazekas, M., Tóth, I. J., & King, L. P. (2012). When government serves the interests of the few: Corruption and state capacity in Hungarian public organisations. *Hungarian Economic Association: Annual Conference 2012*. Budapest: Hungarian Economic Association.

Jancsics, D., & Jávor, I. (2012). Corrupt Governmental Networks. *International Public Management Journal, 15*(1), 62–99. doi:10.1080/10967494.2012.684019

Kaufmann, D., Kraay, A., & Mastruzzi, M. (2007). Growth and Governance: A Reply. *The Journal of Politics, 69*(2), 555–562.

Kaufmann, D., & Vicente, P. C. (2005). *Legal Corruption*.

Kaufmann, D., & Vincente, P. D. (2011). Legal Corruption. *Economics & Politics, 23*(2), 195–219. doi:10.1111/j.1468-0343.2010.00377.x

KPMG. (2012). *EU Funds in Central and Eastern Europe. 2011*. Warsaw, Poland: KPMG.

Kurtz, M. J., & Schrank, A. (2007a). Growth and Governance: Models, Measures, and Mechanisms. *The Journal of Politics, 69*(2), 538–554.

Kurtz, M. J., & Schrank, A. (2007b). Growth and Governance: A Defense. *Journal of Politics, 69*(2), 563–569.

Mungiu-Pippidi, A. et al. (2011). *Contextual Choices in Fighting Corruption: Lessons Learned.* Oslo: Norwegian Agency for Development Cooperation.

Szántó, Z., & Tóth, I. J. (2008). Business corruption in Hungary: From various angles Research summary. Trento.

Szántó, Z., Tóth, I. J., & Varga, S. (2012). The social and institutional structure of corruption: some typical network configurations of corruption transactions in Hungary. In B. Vedres & M. Scotti (Eds.), *Networks in Social Policy Problems.* Cambridge, UK: Cambridge University Press.

Annex 1: Results of regressions on change in total contract value.

Multilevel modelling results for individual companies' change in total contract value before and after the change of government are reported. Our analytical approach is similar to Goldman, Eitan, Jörg Rocholl, and Jongil So. 2013[7] looking at US data. We estimated the coefficients using the following system of equations:

$$Y_{ij} = \beta_{0j} + \beta_{1j} X_{ij} + r_{ij} \tag{1}$$

$$\beta_{0j} = \gamma_{00} + \gamma_{01} Z_{0j} + u_{0j} \tag{2}$$

where Y_{ij} is the logarithm of the difference of total contract value won in 2009 and 2011 by the ith company which operates on jth public procurement market[8], β_{0j} is the constant characterising the jth market, X_{ij} is the characteristics matrix of the ith company operating on the jth market encompassing characteristics such as county of company headquarters, log employment (2009), log turnover (2009), log capital expenditure (2009), and profit margin (2009), r_{ij} stands for the regression error of the company level regressions (first level regressions), γ_{00} is the constant of the market level regressions (second level regressions), Z_{0j} represents the vector characterising the jth market that is market concentration (Hirschman-Herfindahl Index (2009)), and u_{0j} is the error term of the market level regressions.

---

[7] See Goldman, Eitan, Jörg Rocholl, and Jongil So. 2013. "Politically Connected Boards of Directors and The Allocation of Procurement Contracts." Review of Finance, January.

[8] We carried out the logarithmic transformation of the change in contract value according to Goldman et al.: when the difference was positive, we took its logarithm; if it was negative (in 2009 the contracted amount was higher than in 2011) we calculated its absolute value, then took its logarithm, and the resulting value was multiplied by minus one. There were no differences in contract values falling between -1 and +1.

Table 3. Binary logistic regression results

N=27,165 % correct=74.6	dep.var:EU funded/non-EU funded contract				
	B	**Exp(B)**	**S.E.**	**Wald**	**Sig.**
single bidder	0.378	1.46	0.033	130.979	0.000
non-open procedure	0.126	1.134	0.037	11.452	0.001
assessment criteria contains non-price elements	0.204	1.226	0.031	41.825	0.000
contract modified	0.763	2.146	0.04	361.178	0.000
standard submission period (>21 days)				7.703	0.021
accelerated submission deadline (<21 days)	0.081	1.084	0.035	5.227	0.022
extremely short submission deadline (<12 days)	-0.127	0.881	0.096	1.722	0.189
year=2009				21.977	0.000
=2010	0.152	1.165	0.042	13.341	0.000
=2011	0.181	1.199	0.05	13.271	0.000
=2012	0.225	1.253	0.053	17.925	0.000
type of issuer=national				988.649	0.000
=utility	-2.445	0.087	0.138	314.383	0.000
=regional/local	0.222	1.248	0.04	30.563	0.000
=supported agency	1.704	5.495	0.123	190.543	0.000
=body est. by public law	-0.806	0.447	0.058	190.463	0.000
other	-0.306	0.737	0.061	25.109	0.000
missing	-0.78	0.458	0.096	66.341	0.000
market of contract=agriculture&mining				2136.46	0.000
=oil	-4.444	0.012	0.342	169.154	0.000
=food	-2.099	0.123	0.073	832.418	0.000
=clothing	-2.274	0.103	0.314	52.322	0.000
=office&electrical machinery&telecoms	-0.279	0.757	0.066	17.881	0.000
=medical&laboratory	-1.169	0.311	0.065	322.967	0.000
=transport	-1.686	0.185	0.132	162.747	0.000
=defence&security	0.018	1.018	0.223	0.007	0.935
=construction	-0.567	0.567	0.054	108.409	0.000
=IT	-0.428	0.652	0.109	15.454	0.000
=maintenance	-4.191	0.015	0.362	134.002	0.000
=other services	0.975	2.651	0.094	107.865	0.000
=real eastate, finance	-2.198	0.111	0.152	208.44	0.000
=recreation, sports	-0.406	0.666	0.117	11.983	0.001
=utilities&cleaning	-3.687	0.025	0.234	247.474	0.000
=other	-1.158	0.314	0.118	95.481	0.000
log(contract value)	0.246	1.279	0.009	804.627	0.000
constant	-4.327	0.013	0.149	839.494	0.000

Source: MaKAB

7. Bottom of the Heap. The Case of Romania

VALENTINA DIMULESCU, RALUCA POP
AND MADALINA DOROFTEI[1]

The suspension of EU payments in four operational programmes in 2012 showed how problematic Romania's correct and effective management of EU funds is. Such funds aim primarily at decreasing the socio-economic disparities among EU members and support the economic convergence with their Western counterparts of less developed new EU members. Consequently, a poor absorption rate of EU funds threatens income convergence between old and new member countries, thus representing a major challenge for EU integration. Currently, Romania has the poorest absorption rate among all the EU Member States[2] and the worst among the ten new Member States. Moreover, the financial corrections, which amount to roughly 22% of the assimilated European funds, further reduce the real absorption rate, a loss which can be attributed entirely to corruption and mismanagement. The present report investigates the proportion of EU funds which can reasonably be considered at risk because of mismanagement and corruption, asks what are the main defrauding tactics used at national level to obtain European money illicitly, and considers the extent to which the suspension or cancellation of EU assistance might be the best policy for dealing with the situation. In addition, the report will put forward a list of recommendations for the next EU programming period which are intended to mitigate the effects of corruption and mismanagement that result in a waste of public resources.

1. The Problem

Romania is supposed to receive a large amount of EU funding, ranking fourth after Poland, the Czech Republic and Hungary, in terms of the amount earmarked for the 2007-2013 programming period with 19, 67 billion EUR given by the EU for the Convergence and European Territorial Cooperation objectives[3]. At the end of 2012, Romania registered an absorption rate, as measured by the overall payment ratio (intermediary reimbursed payments from the European Commission), of almost 12%[4], dramatically

---

[1] The research was made possible by support from the Think-Tank Fund, Open Society Foundations to the project "Misuse of Public Funds in Romania Before and After EU Accession from 2004 to 2012", implemented by the Romanian Academic Society, the EU 7th Framework Project ANTICORRP, and the authors' voluntary contributions.
[2] Among the underachieving trio, Romania has the lowest absorption rate (as measured by the funds, including the advances, paid by the Commission), totalling 20.7%, in contrast to Italy (28%) and Bulgaria (28.5%).
[3] In Romania, the total sum available for spending, including the national co-financing rate of approximately 5 billion EUR, amounts to 24 billion EUR.
[4] The absorption rate on May 17th, 2013 was 14, 37%, which amounts to a 2.9% rate of increase from December 31st, 2012 (11, 47%).

below Bulgaria (34%), Hungary (40%) and Central and Eastern Europe (CEE) average of 44% (KPMG – CEE, 2013: 9). In addition, among the countries with the lowest contracting ratio, Romania ranks last with 70% as compared to Slovenia (72%), Slovakia (73%) and to the CEE average of 83%. An important indicator of management efficiency in terms of real distribution is the **difference between the grants contracted and those paid** (KPMG – CEE, 2013: 14). The biggest differences are present in Romania (58%) and Bulgaria (66%)[5], the CEE average being 39%.

One of the immediate causes behind the low absorption rate is the decision by the European Commission in 2011 to halt reimbursement claims for two operational programmes (Regional Development and Human Resources) because of problems with the public procurement procedure as pointed out by the Commission's audit missions[6]. The same happened in July 2012 when five operational programmes (Environment, Transport, Human Resources, Economic Competitiveness and Regional Development) were subject to halted reimbursement claims pending the results of the Commission's audit missions[7]. Moreover, at the end of 2012, Romania was subject to pre-suspension mechanisms concerning three operational programmes (Transport, Economic Competitiveness and Regional Development[8]) because of suspicions of fraud and the lack of adequate management and control functions. More precisely, they refer to faulty public procurement procedures, defective financial management and an inadequate prevention and detection practice with regard to fraud and conflict of interest[9]. The direct consequence of all the suspended reimbursements was the fact that the beneficiaries received the funds later than anticipated and the Government had to continue to support the programmes financially either from the state budget[10], or by contracting loans from the international financial market, thus increasing the state deficit.

The **financial corrections** applied by the Commission following audit missions merit special attention because although it has the weakest absorption rate, Romania is subject to the highest level of corrections among all the Member States (Iorga et al., 2013). That particular aspect is analysed in greater detail below.

---

[5] This difference is due to a dramatic increase in the number of contracted funds, Bulgaria managing to attain a 100% contraction rate in 2012, while having a payment rate of 34%.

[6] Popescu, E. (2011) "CE a sistat platile pentru Axa 2 a POR si cere verificarea tuturor contractelor incheiate". *ZiarulFinanciar Daily Newspaper.* 21 June. Available from: <http://www.zf.ro/fonduri-ue/ce-a-sistat-platile-pentru-axa-2-a-por-si-cere-verificarea-tuturor-contractelor-incheiate-8365865/> [Accessed 30/05/2013]; Adevarul (2012) "Cod rosu pe fonduri UE". 23 April. Available from: <http://adevarul.ro/international/europa/cod-rosu-fonduri-ue-1_50ae26f97c42d5a6639a10f1/index.html> [Accessed 30/05/2013]

[7] Sisea, C. (2012) "Orban: Romania nu poate trimite cereri de rambursare pentru patru programme UE". *Ziare.com.* 3 July. Available from <http://www.ziare.com/leonard-orban/ministru-afaceri-europene/orban-romania-nu-poate-trimite-cereri-de-rambursare-pentru-patru-programe-ue-1176632> [Accessed 30/05/2013]

[8] The Human Resources programme was subject to a pre-suspension procedure in August 2012.

[9] For all three programmes, the main shortcomings were found in the management and control systems which are the responsibility of the Management Authority in question. In this sense, the common conclusion was the following: "[t]he Commission considers that there are serious deficiencies in the management and control systems [...] which affect the reliability of the procedure for management verifications and certification of payments for public procurement and for which the corrective measures are not sufficient".

[10] Dan, C. (2012) "Guvernul a transferat temporar 400 milioane lei din privatizari pentru plata proiectelor cu fonduri UE". *Ziarul Financiar Daily Newspaper.* 9 August. Available from: <http://www.zf.ro/fonduri-ue/guvernul-transfera-temporar-400-milioane-lei-din-privatizari-pentru-plata-proiectelor-cu-fonduri-ue-9934634> [Accessed 1/06/2013]

Because of its poor absorption rate which is only slowly increasing, less actual money reaches the ultimate "consumer", the citizen meant to benefit from the financing scheme. The **allocated per capita spending** for Romania – strictly from EU funds – is 897 EUR (if the absorption rate were 100%). Even in that respect Romania lags behind since, according to data from 2012, the **total amount of payments per capita** (155 EUR) is the lowest among the CEE countries (Romanian Fiscal Council, 2012: 43)[11].

The picture described above permits us to state with a degree of certainty that Romania's predicament is a result of a combination of lack of administrative capacity, mismanagement and corruption.

Once political stability seemed to have been achieved in Romania after a stormy year in 2012, structural problems resurfaced. Corruption there remains the worst in the EU-27, echoed by the anti-government slogans of the 2012 demonstrators who stated to their rulers: "We apologize that we cannot produce as much as you can steal"[12]. EU funding absorption is also the lowest, although such funds would be the ideal source of economic recovery for the country. Little work has been done on the association between the two problems and that is the gap the current report tries to fill.

According to a 2012 Eurobarometer survey, 67% of Romanians believe the level of corruption in their country has increased, while 78% of respondents agreed that corruption in Romania is much more pervasive than in other EU Member States[13]. In addition, 79% of Romanians did not believe their government was fighting corruption effectively[14]. The QOG 2-13 ANTICORRP survey (see chapter 8) found that Romanians see a great deal of favouritism and corruption, especially in the law enforcement and health care services.

However, Romania is fighting corruption, but so far each electoral cycle is associated mostly with the prosecution of former government members. In 2012, former Prime Minister Adrian Nastase, a Social Democrat, was imprisoned after many years of being shielded by Parliament against criminal investigation. Nastase is the country's first head of government in the post-communist era to have been convicted of illegally funding presidential election campaign by collecting approximately 1.6 million Euros from companies that declared the payments as attendance fees for a government symposium. The ex-PM fought ferociously, with a dramatic suicide attempt and last-minute tactics to withdraw Government Infrastructure Agency (ISC) complaints from his file, reaching out to ISC director Adrian Balaban-Grajdan, who was later dismissed by his fellow Social Democrat Prime Minister Victor Ponta for his attempt to withdraw the complaint. Nastase was freed for good behaviour in spring 2013 but was dis-

---

[11] Among the lowest absorption rates from this point of view, we find Bulgaria (209 EUR absorbed from 889 EUR allocated per capita) and Slovakia (587 EUR absorbed from 2116 EUR allocated per capita). In contrast, Estonia ranked among the first (1190 absorbed from 2540 EUR allocated per capita) along with Lithuania (1002 EUR absorbed from 2088 EUR allocated per capita).

[12] Wagner, A. (2012) *Corruption and Enlargement in the European Union. Who will limit corruption in Romania Post- Accession?* Presented at the ECSA-C Ninth Biennial Conference, Ottawa, 26-28 April. Available from: <http://canada-europe-dialogue.ca/events/2012-04-ECSA-C-Europe-in-an-Age-of-Austerity/Wagner-CorruptionEnlargementRomania.pdf> [Accessed 03/06/2013]

[13] European Commission (2012) *Special Eurobarometer 374- Corruption* [www]. Available from: <http://ec.europa.eu/public_opinion/archives/ebs/ebs_374_en.pdf> [Accessed 03/06/2013]

[14] Ibid.

missed from the Law Faculty of Bucharest University and is banned from seeking public office. He has further outstanding legal action against him. At the other extreme of the political spectrum, following his government's fall from power in 2012 Sorin Blejnar, the former president of the Agency for Fiscal Administration (ANAF), and the leader of his cabinet Codrut Marta were indicted in September 2012. They were accused of selectively favouring fiscal evasion, and Marta and his wife were charged with organized crime and human trafficking[15]. Blejnar, an appointee of Nastase's foe, President Basescu, made similar claims that the accusations were politically motivated.

This raises the question of how well Romania is controlling corruption? Is corruption the exception in the public funds allocation process, or rather the norm, seeing that Prime Ministers themselves and the heads of tax offices seem to be at the top of this lucrative industry? And how is their general distribution pattern affecting EU funds? As a rule, the discretionary allocation of public funds is a particularly persistent problem in Romania (Mungiu-Pippidi, 2010; Romanian Academic Society, 2011; Institute for Public Policy, 2010 and 2011). The usual illustration is the so-called State Reserve Fund, a national level fund earmarked only for "urgent or unexpected situations" (Article 30, Law 500/2002) and which is annually increased discretionarily without parliamentary approval. Although its amount is established within the State Budget Law of a particular year, the sum is substantially increased through Government decisions, and it is distributed on grounds of political affiliation, not real documented natural emergencies[16]. The main red flags vis-à-vis the management of the fund are the abovementioned increases which are not subject to parliamentary approval and the change in destination from mitigating urgent situations to paying arrears from municipalities[17], the building and/or consolidation of churches or the organisation of film festivals[18].

The general unwritten rule is that most of the money goes to the ruling party or the parties within the ruling coalition (Romanian Academic Society, 2011: 16). **Table 1** below shows the use of the State Reserve Fund over the last four electoral cycles. The clientelism score calculates the ratio between emergency funds allocated to mayors of the government party and the share of the vote for the government party in the given region, all showing significant disproportion until recently. Although all parties in government tend to favour their own mayors, the two centre-right parties when governing by themselves had the highest rate of clientelism. The data indicate that in 2008, the year when the Reserve Fund was increased 509 times above the amount initially allocated (Romanian Academic Society, 2011: 16-17), the clientelism score was at its highest. In 2012, the discrepancies between the allocations for local authorities

---

¹⁵ Romania Curata (2012) *DNA retine 11 persoane in dosarul in care este cercetat si fostul sef ANAF Sorin Blejnar pentru evaziune fiscala*. Available from: <http://www.romaniacurata.ro/dna-retine-11-persoane-in-dosarul-in-care-este-cercetat-si-fostul-sef--3035.htm> [Accessed 30/05/2013]

¹⁶ Popescu, A. (2012) Premierul Ungureanu a mintit: 80% din banii de la fondul de rezerva au mers la primariile Puterii. *Romania Curata*. 10 April. Available from: <http://romaniacurata.ro/ltfont-colorblackgtpremierul-ungureanu-a-mintitlt-fontgtltbrgt-80-din--2681.htm> [Accessed 30/05/2013]

¹⁷ Starting from 2010, this destination took the form of derogations from the Budget Law via Government Emergency Ordinances (GEOs).

¹⁸ Mocanu Chirap, A. (2012) Catedrale si festivale de film din Fondul de Rezerva. Cand inchidem fondurile extrabugetare? *Romania Curata*. 27 March. Available from: <http://romaniacurata.ro/ltfont-colorblackgtcatedrale-si-festivale-de-film-din-fondul-de-rezerv-2622.htm> [Accessed 30/05/2013]

affiliated to government parties and the rest were lower than in previous years and, as a result, the score was the lowest since 2004. However, in 2012 four prime ministers and two parliamentary majorities changed in Romania and it is likely that the resulting political instability affected the trend. The recent improvement of the ratio is due both to a large victory by a left-right alliance – so to a more representative majority – and to a reduction in the volume of the fund due to fiscal crisis.

Table 1: Favouritism in resource allocation trend

Electoral years	2004 (Social Democrats)	2008 (Liberals)	2010 (Liberal Democrats)	2012 (Social Liberal Union)
Preferential allocations made by the main political parties in government (%)	49	45	62	53.67
Votes obtained in local elections (%)	35.5	16.2	28.8	41.57
Clientelism score	**1.4**	**2.8**	**2.2**	**1.3**

Source: Romanian Academic Society, www.sar.org.ro
Legend: State Reserve Fund allocations aggregatd by electoral cycle

The Reserve Fund illustrates how public funds are distributed in Romania in some form of legal corruption. The law is circumvented, funds are distributed to client local governments which further use it to fund locally networked businesses to build churches, repair roads or other frequent public works. For example, far more churches than classrooms have been built in Romania with public funds during the last twenty years. Those businesses then fund the political parties at the local level. The present mechanism of resource allocation and distribution of EU funds by a totally different procedure is a great strain on the Romanian administration.

2. The challenge of documenting corruption

If favouritism is the general rule, with profit being capitalized mostly at party level, individual fraud and corruption are better covered by law and the latter are the subject of most investigations. Relevant data is scarce and favouritism is practically un-documented, but it can be divided into two broad categories: "reported irregularities" (non-fraudulent, suspected fraud, non-confirmed, established fraud[19]) and "related financial amounts". Information pertaining to the two categories was retrieved from the annual reports (2005-2012) written by the Romanian Anti-Fraud Department (DLAF) and the National Anticorruption Directorate (DNA)[20].

---

[19] The data for the "established fraud" sub-category are taken exclusively from the National Anticorruption Directorate's (DNA) annual activity reports.

[20] The DNA has exclusive competence in prosecuting offences against the financial interests of the European Communities (Article 13 of GEO 43/2002).

One caveat related to the figures is that, in the DLAF reports, only in 2012 are the financial amounts related to detected irregularities differentiated in accordance with the affected European financial instrument. Therefore, up to 2012 the data on the number of DLAF detected irregularities include cases pertaining to pre-accession funds, predominantly SAPARD, ISPA and PHARE. As a consequence, we present data from 2005 to 2012 covering two programming periods (**Figures 1** and **2**). In addition, the financial amounts related to the detected irregularities are reported only from 2009 onwards and they are not differentiated between non-fraudulent, suspected fraud and unconfirmed cases. Hence, **Figure 3** presents the related amounts for DLAF investigated irregularities, which include suspected fraud and non-fraudulent cases[21].

From the DNA annual reports we have extracted the number of established fraud cases, namely those which have ended with a definitive legal decision establishing the occurrence of criminal acts. The related financial amounts have been taken from the final court decisions for which such data is made available by the DNA. We also focused on the related sums for the indictments drawn up by the DNA, data which can be assimilated in the "suspected fraud" category, but which contain a stronger indication of foul play. The main limitation of this approach is that it is limited to only those cases which have been investigated successfully, but we are of course aware that the universe of funds subjected to non-random distribution is far higher.

Irregularities refer to cases which were reported as being non-fraudulent, unconfirmed or presenting signs of fraud (**Figure 1**). In addition, the financial amounts are presented vis-à-vis the general category of irregularities and in relation to their number and the sums attached to the indictments drawn up by the DNA from 2009 to 2012, as well as those relating to the final sentences handed down by the courts starting from 2010[22].

Figure 1: Total number of cases with detected irregularities categorized as non-fraudulent, unconfirmed, suspected fraud and established fraud

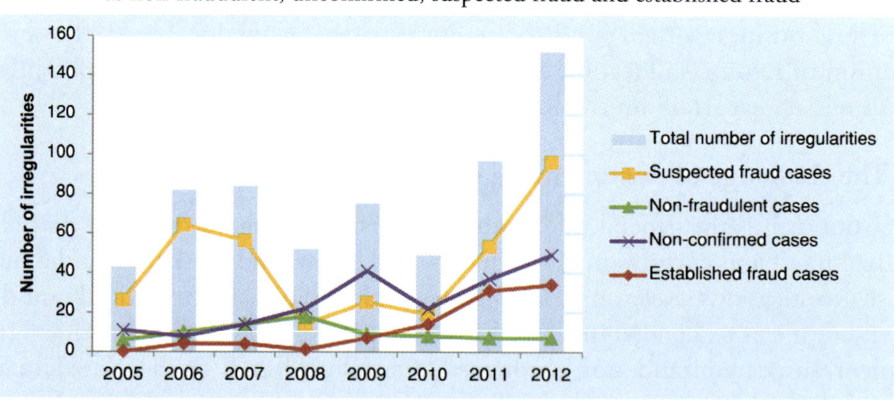

Data sources: DLAF and DNA Annual Activity Reports (2005-2012); author's own computations

---

[21] A FOIA request sent to DLAF by the Romanian Academic Society think tank on June 3rd 2013 through which differentiated data were requested concerning the number of irregularities, suspected fraud, non-fraudulent and non-confirmed cases attached to each European fund from 2005 to 2012 did not yield the expected results because some of the desired indicators did not exist in the DLAF database.

[22] Final sentences establishing the occurrence of acts of fraud and their related financial amounts which have been handed down in cases pertaining to EU funds are publically available on the DNA website starting with the year 2010.

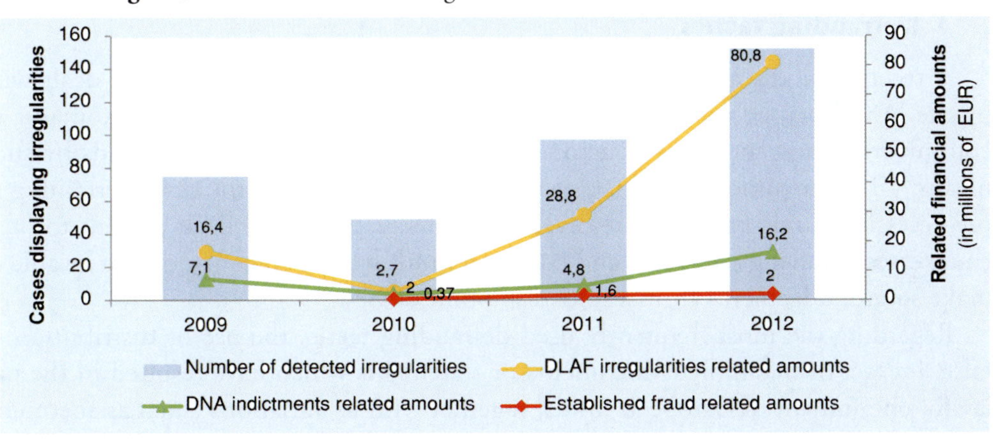

Data sources: DLAF and DNA Annual Activity Reports (2005-2012); author's own computations

Figure 2 points to the fact that from 2005 to 2012 the number of cases with **detected irregularities was** higher than the number of cases reported as **suspected fraud**[23] and **established fraud**. Also, the number of cases of established fraud (convictions handed down by law courts) was considerably lower throughout the same period. However, it should be kept in mind that the number of cases of suspected fraud and established fraud during that period do not refer to the same cases since there is a time lag between the types of irregularities reported by the DLAF and the passing of sentences. Therefore, the majority of established fraud cases refer to pre-accession funding.

Data sources: DLAF and DNA Annual Activity Reports (2005-2012); author's own computations

The data presented in **Figure 3** show that the financial damage attached to detected irregularities (non-fraudulent, non-confirmed, suspected fraud) by DLAF is far higher than the amounts related to the DNA's indictments and to final court decisions establishing the

---

[23] As a result of a FOIA request sent to DLAF by the Romanian Academic Society think tank on June 3rd 2013, the total number of suspected fraud cases between January 2005 and May 2013 was 441.

existence of criminal acts. The total estimated financial damage calculated by DLAF from January 2005 to May 2013 in cases displaying irregularities, including suspicion of fraud, amounts to 243 million Euros[24].

The absolute high was in 2012, when, according to the DLAF, the estimated financial damage was 80 million EUR, which translates to 3.66% of the sum absorbed in the same year (2.2 billion EUR). It should be noted that this sum includes a number of cases referring to pre-accession funding since in the DLAF's annual activity report, no distinction was made between the amounts of pre-accession and post-accession funds.

The **established financial damage** found in court decisions over the last three years is smaller than both the amounts related to detected irregularities and the ones attached to the prosecutors' indictments, but the amount is slowly increasing, which is an indication that instances of fraud are considerably more difficult to prove than to detect. In addition, the amounts proved in court to have been spent illicitly and which need to be recouped may be smaller than the ones initially calculated by the prosecutors and the state authorities. Therefore, a certain amount of money will be lost in this the interaction.

To conclude, with the specific data available *at the present time,* it is clear that the estimated cost of mismanagement and fraud must be considerably higher than the legally proven figures– the majority of which are related to pre-accession funds. We expect that in the years to come all these indicators will show an increase because the cases pertaining to the post-accession period, when available European funds were higher, have not yet been detected or have not yet come to a judicial conclusion.

3. Defrauding tactics

A recent analysis of sentences handed down by courts of law in cases dealt with by the DNA focused on identifying the tactics most frequently used in Romania to commit fraud and the types of actor involved in obtaining European funds by such means[25]. The outcome of the analysis was that, in recent years, the cases pertaining to pre-accession funds have been resolved (Dimulescu, 2013), while at present too few court cases involving structural and cohesion funds have been concluded to be able to make sound judgements from a statistical point of view.

Regarding the most frequently used defrauding tactic, the use or distribution of false, inexact or incomplete documents or statements which have resulted in the unlawful obtainment of European funds, together with its variations (such as abetment, attempt, instigation, improper participation, use of false statements) represented 49.6% of the examined cases. Next most common was the strategy of falsifying documents with 28%. The results are corroborated by the Commission's 2011 Statistical Evaluation of Irregularities, whereby the use of falsified supporting documents (falsified offers)

---

[24] Information obtained as a result of a FOIA request sent to DLAF by the Romanian Academic Society on June 3rd 2013.

[25] The analysis does not present an exhaustive list of defrauding tactics since it concentrated on what could be proven by the DNA prosecutors during the trials ending with definitive sentences.

ranks among the most frequently detected types of infringement concerning pre-accession funds (European Commission, 2012: 71-72).

Figure 4: The frequency of defrauding tactics

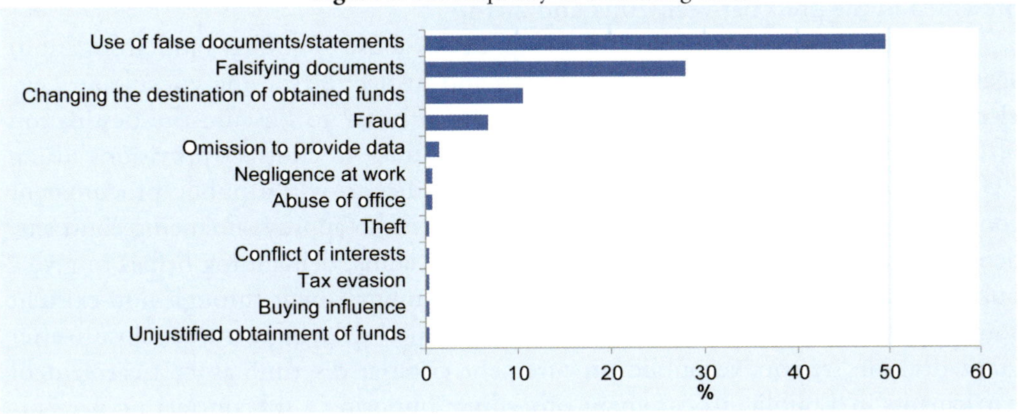

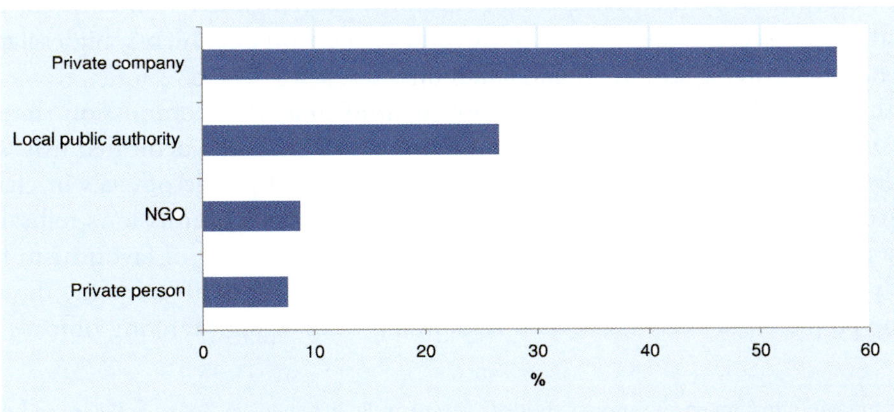

Data source: Dimulescu (2013)

Private firms (associates, administrators, shareholders, executive or administrative directors, managers or employees of private companies) were by far the most often mentioned entity in relation to illicit methods of obtaining EU funds (57.2% of the total). Local public authorities (mayors, vice-mayors, local counsellors and public employees) came second with 26.5%. NGOs (8.7%) and private individuals, mostly farmers and, as often as not, non-existent, (7.5%) completed the list.

The results corroborate the data present in DLAF's 2011 and 2012 annual activity reports on the types of perpetrator since the private sector also came in first in the suspected fraud category (Fight against Fraud Department – DLAF, 2011: 30 and 2012: 36).

Figure 5: Types of entities involved in fraud

Data source: Dimulescu (2013)

The Romanian Academic Society set up a project to monitor press articles both at the local and national level which deal with cases of fraud involving EU money. Their investigation identified a list of 38 methods of fraudulent mismanagement of funds presented in the press between 2004 and 2013.

The list is composed of the following cases: abuse of office (and instigation) against the public interest; accepting bribes(and instigation); using consultancy services throughout the project's implementation in order to obscure the destination of funds; changing the purpose of spending contrary to contract provisions; using EU funds to amass personal benefits; offering bribes to win a public procurement contest; trading political influence with individuals who approve financing contracts; demanding bribes to accept false reimbursement claims; demanding bribes to give a public procurement contract to a certain firm; reimbursement through non-existent companies; following flawed construction techniques; delaying contract closure after grant decision; restrictive public procurement criteria; discriminatory treatment of participants in a public procurement procedure; imposing a subcontracting percentage to the provider of services; the winner of the public procurement contract failing to fulfil conditions necessary for the implementation of a contract; providing invoices to values lower than the true costs incurred; falsification of proof of attainment of a project's intended results and realization of activities; lying about the value of declared indicators; copy/paste evaluation of proposed projects; copy/pasting the contents of a project proposal; tampering with the technical-economic evaluation result; projects written up by consultancy companies favoured by the contracting authority; buying financial statement letters from banks; the use of false, inexact or incomplete documents, statements or falsified certificates; use of bribery to ensure co-financing; disappearing after having received the pre-financing funds; money laundering; additional works declared as being similar activities; conflict of interest; exorbitant amounts used in public procurement contracts administered by certain Management Authorities; delays in finalizing works; omitting to publish the public procurement announcement electronically or publishing it only with a considerable delay so as to favour preferred firms; acceptance by the Management Authority of ineligible reimbursement claims; unauthorized access to a project's control and verification documents; high salaries for project experts although the project's aim does not justify them[26].

The systematic character of the problem is obvious: the Commission stated that one of the reasons for the very slow advancement of the SME dedicated axis was the "widespread collusion between applying companies and public officials in charge of approving applications for funding", the result being the Commission's refusal to receive payment claims[27]. At present, no studies have been made of favouritism for EU funds in Romania. The statistical information that does exist only scratches the surface of the problem but there are several resounding cases of high ranking officials whose

---

[26] For more information on this project entitled "Misuse of Public Funds in Romania Before and After EU Accession", see: <http://sar.org.ro/initiativa-fonduri-europene-manual-de-fraudare/?lang=en>

[27] Pop, R. (2012) De ce si-a pierdut UE increderea in Romania. Ce se intampla cu capacitatea de management si controlul fondurilor europene? *Romania Curata*. 16 November. Available from: <http://www.romaniacurata.ro/articol-3522.htm> [Accessed 05/06/2013]

family or acquaintances have benefitted from a contract with substantial EU funding. For instance, in 2012 a DLAF investigation prompted by a press campaign revealed that in 2011 the Ministry for Rural Development and Tourism, run by Elena Udrea (Liberal Democrats), ignored public procurement rules[28] and gave a publicity contract worth 2 million EUR to the president of the Romanian Boxing Federation who, in turn, "hired" his own private company – which had only 5 part-time employees and until July 2011 had specialized in repairing office equipment– to organize a boxing tournament featuring a well-known Romanian boxing champion[29]. The money were supposed to be used to promote Romania's image as a tourist destination, which was the only eligible activity for reimbursement from the EU, but only 1% of it was used to that end and for 66% of the services provided, the firm did not have the necessary documents (mainly sub-contracting agreements) which were not even requested by the Ministry[30].

Another example is the case of the current Regional Development Minister, Liviu Dragnea (Social Democrats), who in 2009, when he held the office of County Council President of Teleorman County, approved the award of two contracts for road repair to a firm which had been awarded many such public deals in that particular county throughout the years. The firm's owner was one of Dragnea's friends and his brother-in-law later became an MP in Teleorman. An audit investigation from the Commission in 2011 (after which reimbursement claims coming from the Regional Development programme – the axis dealing with the development of local and regional transportation infrastructure – were blocked) revealed that the County Council had imposed restrictive clauses in the public procurement contract which only that particular firm could fulfil[31].

Yet another resonant case occurred in 2011 and involved the Minister of Labour at the time, Ioan Botis (Liberal Democrats). He was investigated by the DLAF, DNA and the National Integrity Agency (ANI) for acts of corruption and conflict of interest pertaining to EU funds. The press revealed that his wife worked for an NGO overseeing a project which had received support through the Human Resources operational programme – which is administered by the Labour Ministry – a month after Botis was appointed head of the same ministry. Moreover, the organisation had its headquarters in the Minister's house, his former chief of parliamentary staff who was also directly involved in the project was one of the NGO's founding members, and the minister's personal assistant and an employee of the ministry received sums of money from the same non-governmental entity. The scandal erupted when Botis himself publically admitted it

---

[28] The attribution of publicity contracts worth more than 20 000 EUR must be preceded by a public procurement participation announcement, be published in the electronic public procurement system and have its own website.

[29] Neag, M., Berceanu, G., And Tolontan, C. (2012) *Comisia Europeana reclama fapte penale la gala organizata de Obreja si finantata de Udrea. Obreja: "Astia de la DLAF se trezesc de dimineata si acuza lumea"*. 26 April. Available from: <http://www.tolo.ro/2012/04/26/comisia-europeana-acuza-fapte-penale-la-gala-organizata-de-obreja-si-finantata-de-udrea/> [Accessed 05/06/2013]

[30] Neag, M., Tolontan, C. (2012) *Cum s-au folosit banii romanilor la Gala Bute: 1% pentru frunza, 99% in vant*. 31 October. Available from: <http://www.tolo.ro/2012/10/31/cum-s-au-folosit-banii-romanilor-la-gala-bute-1-pentru-frunza-99-in-vint/> [Accessed 05/06/2013]

[31] Stoica, I. (2012) Comisia Europeana a descoperit licitatiile truncate ale lui Liviu Dragnea si cere banii inapoi. *EvenimentulZilei*. 14 December. Available from: <http://www.evz.ro/detalii/stiri/liviu-dragnea-se-vrea-ministru-pentru-a-si-albi-licitatiile-trucate-1015760.html> [Accessed 07/06/2013]

to be true, but denied the existence of a conflict of interest[32]. Subsequently, the contract was annulled, the pre-financing sum retrieved and, before a verdict was reached, Ioan Botis resigned from the ministry, although he remained a member of the Labour Committee in the Chamber of Deputies[33].

By aggregating the available data on the number of signed contracts involving EU funds and the political orientation of local authorities, the link between the distribution of contracts and their financial value across political parties can be studied. **Figure 6** presents the number of signed contracts involving structural and cohesion funds at the level of local authorities – meaning county and local councils – from 2007 to September 2011 and show that most contracts (356) were won by officials belonging to the Liberal Democrats (PDL) who were the ruling party at the time. In second place with 336 contracts came the Social Democrats (PSD). The Liberals (PNL) were third with 137, while the ethnic Hungarian party (UDMR) and the Conservatives (PC) came next with 63 and 8 respectively. The financial value of the contracts was high for all the parties involved, but especially for the Liberal Democrats (1, 6 billion EUR) and the Social Democrats (almost 1, 2 billion EUR)[34]. However, the disproportion is less severe than in the case of the Reserve Fund.

Figure 6: Number of signed contracts and their related financial value at the local authority level per political party (2007 – 2011)

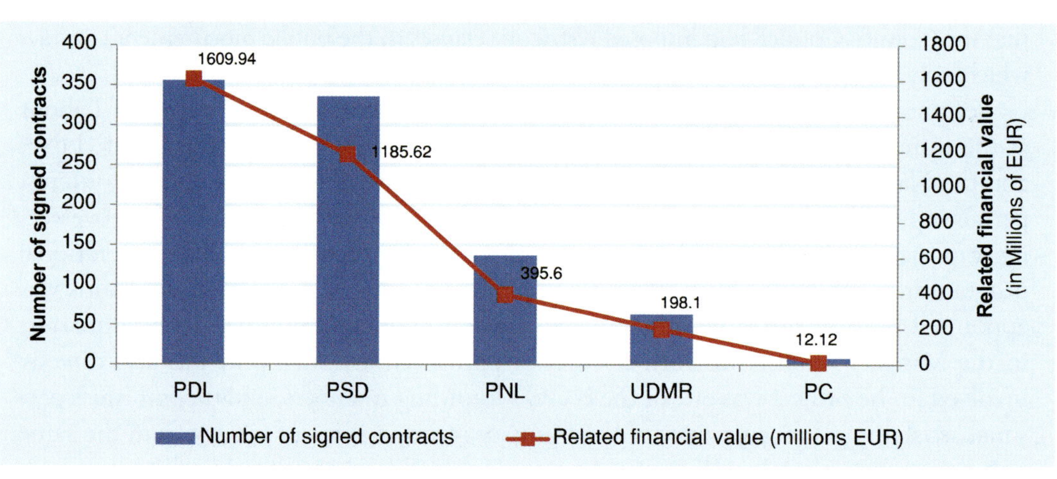

Data sources: Iorga, Alexandru and Ercus (2011); Romanian Academic Society 2013

[32] Mihai, A., Anghel, I. (2011) Cazul Botis ar putea periclita finantarea europeana. *Ziarul Financiar.* 19 April. Available from: <http://www.zf.ro/eveniment/cazul-botis-ar-putea-periclita-finantarea-europeana-8173422> [Accessed 07/06/2013]

[33] Mihai, A. (2011) Asociatia lui Botis trebuie sa inapoieze 150.000 de euro. *Ziarul Financiar.* 18 August. Available from: <http://www.zf.ro/eveniment/asociatia-lui-botis-trebuie-sa-inapoieze-150-000-de-euro-8629124> [Accessed 07/06/2013]

[34] The data include contracts signed only for the following operational programmes: Regional Development, Administrative Capacity Development, Human Resources, Environmental Infrastructure Development and Economic Competitiveness.

4. Financial impact and recommendations

The matter of financial corrections applied by the Commission following audit missions merits particular attention since Romania, as stated above, while showing the lowest absorption rate is subject to the highest level of corrections among all the Member States (Iorga et al., 2013). The corrections refer mainly to deficiencies in the public procurement procedure.

The total amount of imposed corrections from EU accession in 2007 until December 2012 was approximately 300 million EUR[35] – 498 million if we add the 198 million worth of corrections imposed on the Human Resources programme[36]– or 20% to 22.5% of the funds absorbed until the same date (2.2 billion EUR). Furthermore, the most frequent corrections are those amounting to 5% (43% of the cases) and 25% (31% of the cases) of a public procurement contract. The average value of a correction was 13% of a public procurement contract budget (400.000 EUR). The highest corrections targeted the operational programme dealing with regional development (84%), while the second was that dedicated to the environment (13%). Also, the corrections mostly referred to public works contracts (62%), audit services (14%), design activities (7%), technical assistance (6%), consultancy (6%) and publicity services (5%).

The main reasons for their imposition were: illegal qualification requirements (56%), unequal treatment of contenders (11%), the winning offer not fulfilling the conditions (9%), procurement decisions with only one candidate (9%), illegal increase of the contract's value (6%), using the qualification criteria as evaluation factors (6%), ignoring the transparency principle(3%) (Iorga et al., 2013).

The above analysis shows that the estimated direct cost of corruption is small compared to the high opportunity cost posed by poor governance. In that sense development is further curtailed since even the amount of funds absorbed is further drastically reduced by the corrections which resulted from the cases of mismanagement and fraud found both at the beneficiaries' level and within particular national and local state structures entrusted with the management function. The question, therefore, is whether suspension, reduction or cancelling of EU assistance is the most effective mechanism for protecting the interests of the European taxpayer? Or would all of them turn out to be rather like throwing the baby out with the bathwater?

Therefore the **recommendations** for better management of European funds in Romania for the 2014-2020 programming period should focus on pre-emption or ex-ante controls so as to avoid reaching the stage where the funds are suspended, reduced or cancelled– a situation which does not fully resolve the problem since the money cannot be recouped in full by the EU through corrections. Therefore, this report suggests the following:

---

[35] The financial correction was greater than that of Spain (158 million), Poland (24 million) or Germany (22 million). The Institute for Public Policy's study did not look at the financial corrections imposed on the Human Resources programme at the end of 2012.

[36] Preluca, R. (2012) Memorandum privind corectiile pe POSDRU, aprobat astazi de Guvern, *fonduri-structurale.ro*. 27 November. Available from: <http://www.fonduri-structurale.ro/detaliu.aspx?eID=12078&t=Stiri> [Accessed 08/06/2013]

1. **The creation of an Early Warning mechanism to pre-empt the suspension of funds.** More specifically, a mechanism is needed by means of which the verification and control procedure is made more efficient *before* the suspension or cancellation of EU assistance comes into effect. To that end, there needs to be a set of indicators used to give early warning of the suspicion of fraud or irregularity not only at the public procurement and project selection level, but at project level too. Such indicators could be grouped according to the phase of the project's life-cycle (definition of grants conditions and terms of reference, grant/procurement decision, implementation of the project/grant and general, systemic conditions).

2. **The design of a system of social accountability in monitoring and auditing the spending of EU funding.** This recommendation refers to entrusting direction of every stage of projects (planning, evaluation and audit) to local stakeholders, in other words to those who stand to lose most from corrupt use of EU funds, so enhancing transparency and control. The system would be based on precise information given by different community or sector stakeholders and which would allow various outcomes. First, it would facilitate swift monitoring to allow quick reactions from journalists and civil society. Second, it would allow pre-emptive actions from managing authorities and thus deter the suspension of EU structural and cohesion funds. Third, it would bring more transparency to the management system and reduce incentives to fraudulent activity. The innovative aspect of the output will be its reference to the role different stakeholders will be able to play in the monitoring of the spending of EU structural and cohesion funds: the press, civil society, beneficiaries, public procurement competitors, evaluators, consultants, personnel in the management and control system and the directly responsible public authorities.

3. **The development of a more inclusive, participatory process of design, monitoring and implementation for the next programming period.** The result of Romania's absorption history is the existence of a group of people who possess sufficient training and expertise to recommend better avenues for efficient spending. They are familiar with both the pre-accession programme and the current framework, some of them having gained experience in areas as vast as evaluation, consultation, project implementation and programme management. They could become part of an Expert Consultation/Monitoring Group and would be able to contribute to better decision-making, as well as being capable of analysing fraudulent practices and discussing solutions for them. This group could complement the local stakeholders' involvement with the necessary insight to disentangle the hindrances – both intentional and unintentional – to a proper and efficient spending of EU funds. More specifically, such individuals have access to technical or legal information out of the reach of local stakeholders, but in Romania such experts and practitioners are seldom encouraged to take part in the refinement of public procurement and management practices of EU funds.

In the current format, they are discouraged from expressing any negative views since that would be interpreted as unsolicited critical opinion. More openness from the Management Authorities and the Ministry of European Funds would send an encouraging signal in that regard. Therefore, participation in monitoring activities and the positive channelling of dissent could be transformed into a prestigious and well-received activity.

4. **Improvement in the quality of evaluation and enhancement of the personal responsibility of independent evaluators contracted by operational programme managers.** Much fraud happens because of bad project or contract *evaluation*. If a project is too vague or is badly written but has passed the evaluation stage, it can be argued that a missing objective – absent due perhaps to miss-spending or fraud – has in fact been achieved. Basically, once a contract or a project has been accepted, the monitoring institutions, civil society, stakeholders and the media can report only those instances where the money requested and the money spent do not contribute to achieving the agreed outcomes, outputs and specific objectives found in the project application. The evaluation step is critical in the sense that it legitimizes the project and subsequent claims for reimbursement. Therefore, the concrete recommendation is the following: improve the quality of evaluation so as to limit the number of projects which could be defrauded due to badly written project-applications and inflated project costs. That can be done by increasing the personal responsibility given to individual evaluators, but also by increasing transparency to the general public about the projects funded and offering them information such as specific objectives, main activities, expected results, duration of the project, and so on.

References

Dimulescu, V. (2013) Private firms surpass the local authorities in defrauding European funds. *Romanian Academic Society.* [online] 9th April. Available from: http://sar.org.ro/wp-content/uploads/2013/04/RAS-analysis_Defrauding-of-EU-funds-in-Romania.pdf

European Commission (2012) EU cohesion funding – key statistics. Percentage of funds allocated per MS paid by the Commission, *on the basis of claims submitted. [online]*8th November. *Available from:*http://ec.europa.eu/regional_policy/thefunds/funding/index_en.cfm

European Parliament (2012) *Statistical Evaluation of Irregularities reported for 2011. Own Resources, Natural Resources, Cohesion policy, Pre-Accession and Direct Expenditure.*SWD(2012) 229 final. European Commission. Brussels. [online] Available from: http://eur-lex.europa.eu/LexUriServ/LexUriServ.do?uri=SWD:2012:0229:FIN:EN:PDF

Fight Against Fraud Department – DLAF (2005-2012) Annual Activity Reports. Available from: http://www.antifrauda.gov.ro/ro/despre_noi/rapoarte/

KPMG – CEE (2013) EU Funds in Central and Eastern Europe – Progress Report 2007-2012. *KPMG Warsaw.* [online] Available from:http://uelive.ro/wp-content/uploads/2013/05/EU-Funds-in-Central-and-Eastern-Europe-%E2%80%93-Progress-report-2007-2012.pdf

Iorga, E.et al. (2013) Note de constatare a neregulilorsi de stabilire a corectiilorfinanciare in proiectele cu finantare din fonduri structural financiare.*Institute for Public Policy, Roma-*

nian Municipalities' Association. [online] April. Available from: http://www.ipp.ro/library/IPPconcluziicorectii.pdf

Iorga, E., Alexandru, V. And Ercus, L. (2011) Structural Funds – from a development opportunity to a preyed upon budget.Part 1.*Institute for Public Policy.* [online] 21st July. Available from: http://www.ipp.ro/pagini/fondurile-structurale-de-la-oportunita.php

Iorga, E., Alexandru, V. And Ercus, L. (2011) Structural Funds – from a development opportunity to a preyed upon budget.Part 2.*Institute for Public Policy.* [online] 28th September. Available from: http://www.ipp.ro/pagini/fondurile-structurale-de-la-oportunita-1.php

Institute For Public Policy (2010) Political clientelism has bankrupted not only the State Budget, but also local communities. [online] 4th June. Available from: http://www.ipp.ro/pagini/clientelismul-politic-a-falimentat-nu-nu.php

Institute For Public Policy (2011) The money from the State Reserve are distributed based on political criteria. [online] 5th January. Available from: http://www.ipp.ro/pagini/banii-din-rezerva-guvernului-sunt-trimi.php

Institute For Public Policy (2011) By deciding upon the Reserve Fund, the Government plays the role of Parliament. IPP asks the Parliament to claim its sovereign right to decide the destination of public spending. [online] 29th November. Available from: http://www.ipp.ro/pagini/prin-deciziile-privind-fondul-de-rezerv.php

National Anticorruption Directorate (2005-2012) Annual Activity Reports. Available from: http://www.pna.ro/faces/results.xhtml

Mungiu-Pippidi, A. (2010) A Case Study in Political Clientelism. Romania's Policy-Making Mayhem.*World Bank functional review report on Romania.* Available from:http://sar.org.ro/wp-content/uploads/2012/01/A-Case-Study-in-Political-Clientelism-Romania-Policy-Making-Mayhem.pdf;

Romanian Academic Society (2011) Beyond perception: Has Romania's governance improved after 2004?*RAS Policy analysis and forecast report for 2011.* [online] 25th February. Available from:http://sar.org.ro/wp-content/uploads/2012/12/Annual-Policy-Report-RAS-2011.pdf

Romanian Fiscal Council (2012) Annual Report for 2011 – Macroeconomic and budgetary evolutions and perspectives. [online] Available from: http://www.consiliulfiscal.ro/Raport2011.pdf

8. European Perceptions of Quality of Government: A Survey of 24 Countries

NICHOLAS CHARRON

This report outlines the results of a recent survey within the ANTICORRP project[1], a survey intended to capture the 'quality of government' (QOG) – e.g. quality, level of corruption (perceived and experienced) and the extent to which public services are allocated impartially in 20 EU countries Turkey, Serbia, and Ukraine[2]. The purpose of the survey is to aid scholars, practitioners and policy-makers interested in going beyond comparisons and analyses at the national level, and to compare QoG across and within countries. Thus the survey focuses primarily – yet not exclusively - on public services such as education, health and law enforcement, which are often administered by sub-national authorities.

The questions were aimed at the consumers of everyday public services – ordinary European residents – to which over 400 responded per NUTS 1 or 2 regions (Nomenclature of territorial units for statistics). With a total sample of more than 85,000 respondents, it is currently the largest multi-country governance survey aimed at capturing regional variation and its explanations. Questions focus not only on perceptions, but also on citizens' experience of services and their level of satisfaction, as well as on individual opinions regarding quality of public services, media, elections, social trust and the perceived and experienced meritocracy of the public and private sector.

Content and Past Research

This report highlights the findings of the survey, and for practical reasons of space, the results are mainly those from the national level. However, the data will be published freely at both the individual level and aggregated regional level, thus users may take the level of analysis that most suits their research needs. The following is a descriptive report and not an analytical one, thus the 'why' questions (why certain countries or regions rate higher in QoG than others) are left for future research.

This survey builds on a pilot project from 2010, sponsored by the EU Commission (REGIO), entitled 'Measuring Quality of Government and Sub-National Variation (Charron, Lapuente and Rothstein, 2010), whereby 34 QoG oriented and demographic questions were posed to 34,000 EU respondents in 172 NUTS regions in 18

---

[1] For more information about the ANTICORRP project, see: <http://anticorrp.eu/>

[2] Serbia includes Kosovo and Ukraine is limited to only six regions.

countries. The project was ultimately intended to build a regional QoG composite indicator, which was subsequently called the EQI (*European Quality of Government Index* – Charron, Dijkstra and Lapunte 2013; Charron, Lapuente and Rothstein 2013). The EQI for 2013 and its methodology will be published in a separate document; however it will primarily build on the 2010 round.

In addition to what was asked in the 2010 round, the current survey adds several questions – including questions about social trust, meritocracy within the public and private sector, left-right voter ideology, perceived 'greed corruption' in society, and the consequences for political parties linked to corruption scandals, all of which are summarized in this report.

This report is structured in the following way:

1. Sample: countries and regions included
2. Methodology
3. Expert Summary
4. Detailed description of the respondents: demographics in general and by country and
5. Respondents' experience with public services in question in the last 12 months
6. Perceived and experienced quality of 3 public services: education, health care and law enforcement
7. Perceived and experienced impartiality of three public services: education, health care and law enforcement
8. Perceived and experienced corruption in three public services: education, health care and law enforcement. Perceived corruption of the extent to which 'greed corruption' occurs
9. Perceived corruption in elections, and public trust in media reporting of political and bureaucratic corruption
10. Level of social trust and perceived and experienced level of meritocracy in the public and private sectors
11. Consequences for political parties in corruption scandals.

1. Sample

All countries in the EU28 with multiple NUTS 2 regions are included, along with Turkey, Serbia (including Kosovo), and parts of Ukraine.

Table 1

Abreviation	Countries at NUTS 1 level	No. of Regions	No. of total respondents
DE	Germany	16	6400
UK	United Kingdom	12	4800
SE	Sweden	3	1295
BE	Belgium	3	1208
HU	Hungary	3	1215
GR	Greece	4	1613
TR	Turkey	12	4800
	Countries at NUTS 2 level		
IT	Italy	21	8500
DK	Denmark	5	2028
FI	Finland	5	2000
NL	Netherlands	12	4822
AT	Austria	9	3600
CZ	Czech Republic	8	3236
SK	Slovakia	4	1609
ES	Spain	17	6800
PT	Portugal	7	2886
FR	France	26	10409
PL	Poland	16	6400
RO	Romania	8	3200
BG	Bulgaria	6	2402
HR	Croatia	2	800
IE	Ireland	2	800
RS	Serbia*	5	2015
UA	Ukraine	6	2400
Total	24 countries	212	85238

* Serbia includes Kosovo as the EU does not recognize Kosovo as fully sovereign. However, we have highlighted the results of Kosovo separately in this report. Kosovo as a region in the survey has 400 total respondents.
** EU15 refers to the 15 countries forming the European Union before the enlargements of 2004 and 2007. EU 15 countries (12): BE, AT, DE, SE, DK, IE, FR, NL, ES, PT, GR, UK
*** The NMS13 are the 13 'new Member States' which joined the European Union during the 2004 and 2007 Enlargements as well as Croatia in 2013. NMS13 countries (7): RO, PL, BG, SK, HU, CZ, HR
**** Includes an ascending state (Turkey), a potential candidate (Serbia) and 6 of the 24 oblasts from Ukraine. Non-members (3): RS, TR, UA

2. Methodological Issues

The surveys were initiated during the month of February, 2013 and were conducted in the local majority language of each country/region. The results were returned to the Quality of Government Institute in April, 2013.

This project consists of a large international survey conducted via telephone interviews, each of approximately 10 minutes during which 32 questions were posed. The sample size of citizens in the survey was over 85,000 Europe-wide, with the final focus of the collected data aimed at the regional level. The survey selectively sampled 400-plus citizens per region, so the sample size for each country varies depending on the number of regions. The regional level for each country in the survey is based on the European Union's NUTS[3] statistical regional level and is as follows for the countries in the survey. The NUTS level for each country was selected with two factors in mind – the extent to which elected political authorities have administrative, fiscal or political control over one or more of the public services in question, and two, the cost of the service to the consumer. In direct consultation with the EU Commission, the NUTS regions shown in the previous section in each country were selected on those basic criteria.

The public services in question – education, health care and law enforcement - were selected instead of nationally administered services such as immigration, customs, the armed forces or courts in order to maximize regional variation in the QoG-oriented question in the survey.

We also had to consider the great variation of powers and competencies across European regions. In some countries, such as Germany, Belgium, Italy or Spain we deal with political and legislative regions, while in others the region is simply an administrative unit. 'Political' regional governments are elected by their local constituents and such governments have their own autonomous revenues and a degree of fiscal and policy autonomy. In unitary government countries however, such as Bulgaria, Romania, Slovakia or Portugal we target regions which are sometimes not even fully fledged administrative units, (NUTS 1 or NUTS 2), but statistical creations designed for EU cohesion funds. Therefore in some cases asking a respondent 'how would you rate the quality of this or that service 'X' in your particular administrative region "Y' might be very confusing, since respondents from countries like Hungary or Romania might not even be aware that they are even living in region 'Y' which is only a vehicle for the distribution and management of EU regional and cohesion funds. It can therefore be argued that the administrative and political responsibility of the regions in the three public services we have chosen to concentrate on varies in different countries, which might cause problems with the gathering of our data. However this study argues otherwise, in that we attempt to capture all regional variation within a country and as several other scholars have noted (e.g. Tabellini 2005) there are numerous empirical indications and anecdotal evidence that the provision and quality of public services controlled by a powerful central government can nonetheless vary greatly across different regions.

Thus to synthesize the survey and make the results as comparable as possible within and between countries, we asked respondents questions focusing on three key concepts

---

[3] For more information on the NUTS system, please see: <http://epp.eurostat.ec.europa.eu/portal/page/portal/nuts_nomenclature/introduction>

of QoG – the 'quality' of the actual services, the extent to which they are administered 'impartially' and the extent to which 'corruption' exists *in their area.*

The EU regional survey was undertaken between 20 February, 2013, and 6 April, 2013 by Efficience 3 (E3), a French market research company specializing in gathering information about public opinion throughout Europe tailored to the needs of researchers, politicians and advertising firms. E3 conducted the interviews themselves in certain of the countries and used sub-contracting partners in others[4]. The respondents, all 18 years old or more, were contacted at random in the local language via the telephone.

Ideally, a survey would be a mirror image of actual societal demographics – gender, income, education, rural-urban, and so on. However, we are not privy to exact demographic distributions, especially not at the regional level, so that if we had imposed artificial demographic boundaries we might well have met problems greater than any benefits we might have gained. So we sought the next best solution. Based on E3's expert advice, to achieve a random sample we used what is known in the business of survey-research as the 'next birthday method', which is an alternative to the so-called quotas method. When using the quota method for instance, one obtains an almost perfectly representative sample – a nearly exact proportion of, for example, the number of men; or women, certain minority groups, people of a certain age, income, or whatever it might be. However, as the search narrows to certain demographics within the population, one might end up with only 'available' respondents, or those who are more 'eager' t o respond to surveys, which can lead to less variation in the responses, or even to bias in the results. The 'next-birthday' method, which simply requires the interviewer to ask the person who answers the phone who in their household will be the next one to celebrate his or her birthday, still obtains a reasonably representative sample of the population. The interviewer must then deal with the member of the household who will next pass a birthday, and if that individual is not immediately available the interviewer must make an appointment. By that means the survey need not rely on whoever might happen to be available to respond at the time of the telephone call. So, although the quota method is stronger in terms of a more even demographic spread in the sample, the next-birthday method is better at ensuring a wider range of opinion. Therefore we chose the next-birthday method because we felt that what we might have lost in demographic representation in the sample would be made up for by a more satisfactory distribution of opinion.

Therefore we chose the next-birthday method because we felt that what we might have lost in demographic representation in the sample would be made up for by a more satisfactory distribution of opinion.

In total, more than 85,200 respondents across Europe took part in the survey. A complete demographic profile can be found on the online version of this report on www.anticorrp.eu . The majority of respondents come from a city or town with fewer than 100,000 residents, which is not especially surprising because the NUTS region, not the coun¬try, was the focus and the majority of such regions contain no major city. Although numbers varied somewhat among the countries, the distribution of

---

[4] <http://www.efficience3.com/en/accueil/index.html>. For names of the specific firms to which Efficience 3 sub-contracted in individual countries, please write cati@efficience3.com

respondents by age was well represented – roughly 18% were under 30, 36% were from 30-49, 27% were from 50-64 and 19% were 65 or older. A little more than 18% were employed in some capacity in the public sector, while roughly 35% worked in the private sector. Almost 36% were either retired, in education, or worked at home as housewives or househusbands. 8.3% answered that they were currently unemployed. 26% were lower income earners, 31% were in their country's respective 'middle range', while about 29% were at the higher end. Roughly 13% across the whole sample either did not know or refused to give the information.

3. Experience of Primary Public Services in Question

In the first three questions, respondents were asked simply if they or anyone in their immediate family had had personal contact with any or all of the three primary public services in question.

Q1. *Have you or any of your immediate family been enrolled or employed in the public school system in your area in the past 12 months? (yes, no)*

Q2. *In the past 12 months have you or anyone in your immediate family used public health care services in your area? (yes, no)*

Q3. *Have you or anyone in your immediate family had any recent contact (positive or negative) with the security or police forces in your area in the past 12 months? (yes, no)*

Generally speaking, we found that more than 88% of respondents had had direct contact with at least one of the three primary services in question, while 44% had had direct contact with two or more and about 9.5% had had direct contact with all three over the preceding year. Only 11.8% had had no contact with any of the three.

Figure 1. Direct Experience with Public Services

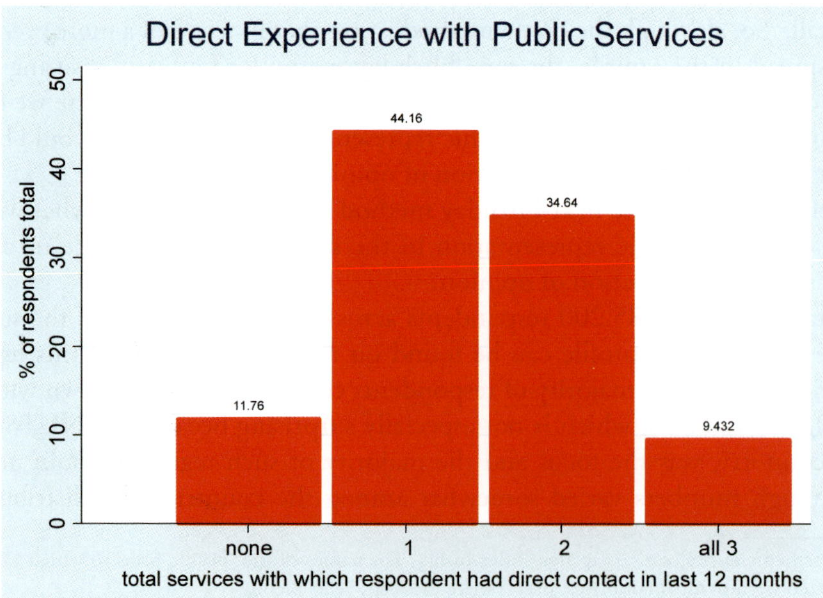

Looking at results for each service individually and within countries, we find some variation across the services themselves as well as across countries. Approximately 39% of respondents had direct contact with their area's education services over the preceding 12 months, with lowest rate of experience in the Kosovo region, Greece and Sweden while a majority of respondents in Ukraine, Hungary and Bulgaria had had direct contact with their area's public education services.

Figure 2. Encounters with Education Services

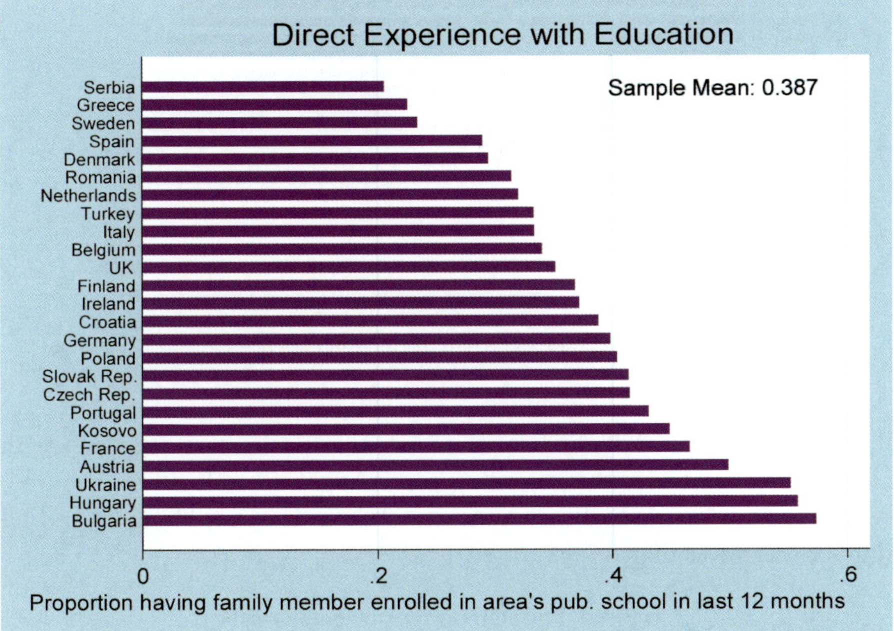

The vast majority of all respondents had had direct contact with their health care services in the last 12 months (about 82%), and in all countries a strong majority of respondents had been in direct contact with the health care services in their area.

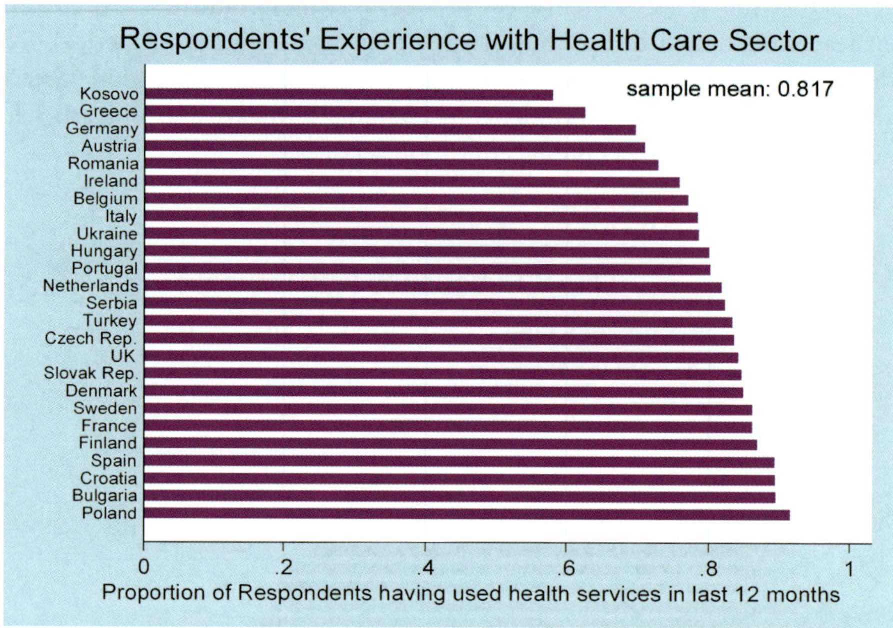

Figure 3. Encounters with Health Services

Of the whole sample 22% had contact - whether positive or negative - with their area's law enforcement over the preceding year. Approximately 30% or more in Belgium, Croatia and Austria had such contact, while in Kosovo, Hungary and Ukraine the number was fewer than 17%.

Figure 4. Encounters with Law Enforcement

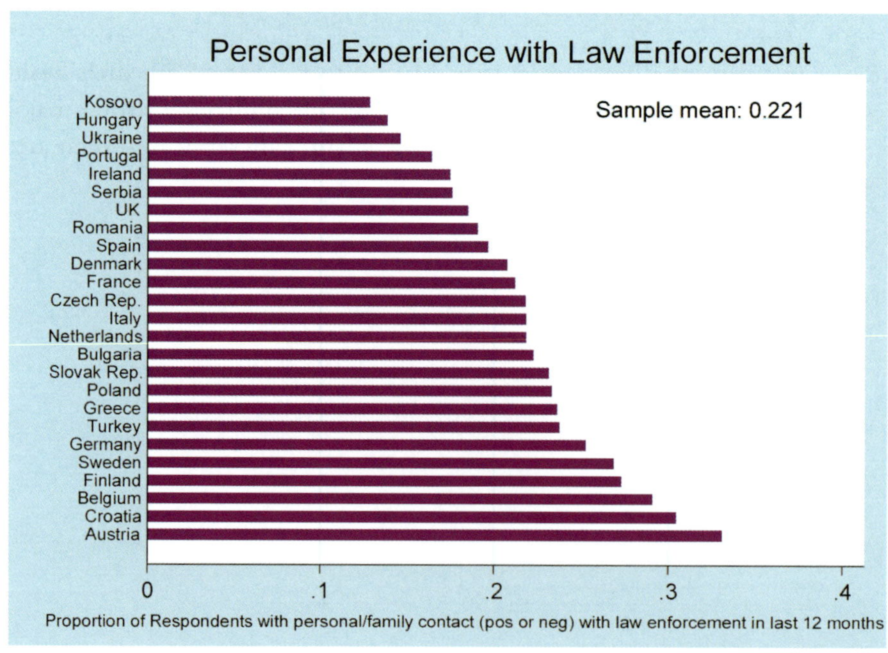

4. Perceived and experienced quality of 3 public services: education, health care and law enforcement

In question 4-6, respondents were asked to rate the quality of their three services. The following was read out to them:

Questions 4-6 deal with your opinion of the quality of services in your area, please rate the following from (0-10, with '0' being very poor and '10' being excellent quality)

Q4. "How would you rate the quality of public education in your area?"

Q5. "How would you rate the quality of the public health care system in your area?"

Q6. "How would you rate the quality of the police force in your area?"

In **Table 2**, we show simple aggregated country averages along with the simple aggregated averages for the respondents with and without direct experience of them for each of the three services by country. We can see in all but two cases (Turkey and Croatia) that those who have direct experience of education services in their area generally rate the services more highly than those with no experience of them. The largest gap between quality ratings by those with experience as against those without is in Ukraine, Romania and Bulgaria, while in Finland and Croatia the gap is negligible. In all countries, the average response is above '5', suggesting that most Europeans are generally satisfied with the quality of education services.

For health care, the average respondent with direct experience generally perceived the services to be of higher quality than did those without, with the exception of Kosovo. Respondents in Belgium, the Netherlands and Finland rate their health care most highly while it is rated lowest in Greece, Kosovo and Ukraine. When looking at law enforcement we see that throughout Europe citizens rate the service generally positively, with an aggregate above '5'. However, the pattern changes when we compare those with experience and those without. In all but 7 countries, those with direct experience generally rate the quality of the services lower than those without direct experience. The gap between respondents with and without experience is widest in Turkey, Serbia and Romania. Overall, the quality of law enforcement is rated highest in Finland, Denmark and Romania, and lowest in Ukraine, Bulgaria and Poland.

Table 2. Quality of Public Services, Total and by Experience

Country	Education			Health Care			Law Enforcement		
	experience	no experien	total	experience	no experien	total	experience	no experien	total
1 AT	6.77	6.32	6.54	6.94	6.37	6.78	6.72	6.4	6.51
2 BE	7.11	6.85	6.94	7.57	7.36	7.52	6.38	6.83	6.71
3 BG	5.5	4.9	5.25	4.81	4.42	4.77	5.54	5.31	5.36
4 CZ	6.67	6.19	6.39	6.42	6.01	6.35	6.14	6.16	6.16
5 DE	6.66	6.07	6.3	6.77	6.28	6.62	6.65	6.36	6.43
6 DK	6.89	6.44	6.58	7.04	6.84	7.01	6.87	6.81	6.82
7 ES	6.56	6.38	6.43	6.66	6.47	6.64	6.24	6.54	6.48
8 FI	7.73	7.54	7.61	7.1	6.67	7.05	7.29	7.16	7.2
9 FR	6.7	6.32	6.5	6.76	6.54	6.73	5.97	6.29	6.22
10 GR	6.26	5.72	5.84	4.64	4.46	4.57	6.42	6.13	6.2
11 HR	6.11	6.15	6.14	5.97	5.81	5.96	5.65	6.16	6
12 HU	6.6	6.28	6.46	6.07	5.76	6.01	5.71	6.49	6.38
13 IE	7.38	7.03	7.16	6.59	5.85	6.41	6.39	6.41	6.41
14 IT	6.71	6.49	6.56	6.31	5.99	6.24	6.81	6.82	6.81
15 KO	5.86	5.4	5.6	4.62	4.67	4.63	6.06	6.78	6.68
16 NL	7.12	6.63	6.8	7.46	7.24	7.42	6.6	6.7	6.68
17 PL	6.46	6.13	6.27	4.97	4.59	4.94	5.59	5.98	5.87
18 PT	6.86	6.34	6.58	6.14	5.54	6.02	6.12	6.21	6.19
19 RO	7.22	6.63	6.82	6.28	5.92	6.18	6.07	6.95	6.78
20 RS	5.88	5.72	5.76	5.46	5.24	5.43	5.25	6.18	6.01
21 SE	6.32	5.91	6.01	6.64	6.1	6.57	6.73	6.49	6.55
22 SK	6.07	5.91	5.97	5.26	5.21	5.25	5.47	5.98	5.86
23 TR	5.45	5.81	5.69	6.39	5.94	6.32	5.66	6.57	6.35
24 UA	6.36	5.58	6.01	4.78	4.74	4.77	4.11	4.58	4.51
25 UK	7.06	6.53	6.72	6.9	6.54	6.84	6.42	6.45	6.44

Note: answer ranges from 0-10, with higher numbers equating to higher rated quality.

5. Perceived and experienced impartiality of 3 public services: education, health care and law enforcement

Q7-9: Please respond to the following 3 questions on a scale of 0-10, with 0 being 'strongly disagree' and 10 being 'strongly agree'

Q7. "Certain people are given special advantages in the public education system in my area."

Q8. "Certain people are given special advantages in the public health care system in my area."

Q9. "The police force gives special advantages to certain people in my area."

In **Table 3**, the trends between those with experience and those without are less obvious across countries. In some cases, respondents without direct experience rated their services as more impartial than those with experience (Austria for education and health care for example) while in other cases, those with direct contact rated the services more impartial on average than the respondents without direct contact (Hungary for education and health care for example). With respect to the gap in impartiality ratings between those with experience and those without, only in Austria and Kosovo do we see that those with direct contact in the past year rate the service as more impartial than those without direct contact.

Concerning impartiality, on the whole responses varied across countries and across services. Generally speaking, health care is seen as the service where certain citizens are given certain advantages when compared with education or law enforcement. In Finland, Sweden, the Netherlands and Ireland, services are rated as quite impartial across the board, while in Ukraine, Kosovo, Croatia and Serbia they are seen as giving advantages to certain people throughout the public sector. In some countries, only certain services are rated as relatively partial (France with health care, or Greece with law enforcement) while others are seen as relatively impartial.

Table 3. Favouritism/Impartiality Public Services, Total and by Experience

Country	Education			Health Care			Law Enforcement		
	total	experience	no experience	total	experience	no experience	total	experience	no experience
1 AT	4.24	4.44	4.04	4.68	4.88	4.18	3.43	3.36	3.47
2 BE	5.07	4.77	5.23	5.4	5.39	5.45	4.61	4.99	4.44
3 BG	3.96	3.82	4.16	5.12	5.15	4.91	4.9	5.03	4.86
4 CZ	4.43	4.31	4.52	5.14	5.17	5.01	4.54	4.97	4.42
5 DE	3.77	3.65	3.84	4.53	4.52	4.57	3.08	3.19	3.04
6 DK	3.93	3.81	3.99	4.17	4.22	3.93	2.88	3.08	2.82
7 ES	4.46	4.34	4.51	4.63	4.61	4.79	4.5	4.71	4.45
8 FI	3.47	3.39	3.52	3.78	3.81	3.65	2.64	2.64	2.64
9 FR	4.92	4.92	4.93	5.35	5.34	5.38	4.55	4.65	4.52
10 GR	4.54	4.57	4.53	4.69	4.74	4.6	5	5.3	4.91
11 HR	6.07	5.98	6.13	6.68	6.68	6.7	6.08	6.19	6.03
12 HU	4.13	3.98	4.33	4.75	4.67	5.07	3.88	4.4	3.79
13 IE	3.7	3.38	3.89	3.89	3.96	3.7	3.56	3.37	3.6
14 IT	3.89	3.73	3.97	4.87	4.91	4.68	3.61	3.8	3.56
15 KO	6.22	6.26	6.2	6.35	6.21	6.53	5.51	5.44	5.49
16 NL	3.79	3.63	3.88	3.58	3.53	3.81	3.13	3.47	3.03
17 PL	4.41	4.37	4.44	5.41	5.4	5.52	3.9	4.25	3.78
18 PT	4.88	4.84	4.91	5.25	5.26	5.24	4.8	5.15	4.73
19 RO	4.24	4.19	4.26	4.96	4.95	5	4.4	4.92	4.28
20 RS	6.09	5.89	6.14	6.56	6.53	6.68	6.3	6.41	6.28
21 SE	3.44	3.48	3.42	3.57	3.56	3.56	2.8	2.92	2.75
22 SK	5.2	5.32	5.11	6.2	6.27	5.85	5.68	5.91	5.61
23 TR	4.03	4.29	3.9	3.75	3.6	4.53	3.82	4.46	3.61
24 UA	6.1	6.01	6.21	6.57	6.7	6.1	6.73	7.54	6.59
25 UK	4.28	4.19	4.33	4.17	4.14	4.32	3.78	3.96	3.74

Note: answer ranges from 0-10, with lower numbers equating to greater levels of impartiality.

As impartiality is generally a more abstract concept than 'quality' or even 'corruption', we elected to re-phrase the question 'in the positive' so to speak, so as to best capture the respondents' conception of impartiality. That was done as follows in questions 10 to 12.

Q10-12: Please respond to the following 3 questions with 'Agree, rather agree, rather disagree or Disagree'

Q10. "All citizens are treated equally in the public education system in my area"

Q11. "All citizens are treated equally in the public health care system in my area"

Q12. "All citizens are treated equally by the police force in my area"

In most cases, the numbers are generally consistent with the previous three questions – Sweden, Finland, Denmark, the Netherlands and Ireland tend to view their services unreservedly as impartial, while in Ukraine, Greece, Slovakia and Serbia on average they are seen as favouring certain people. Some noticeable differences were found in Spain and Romania, where the respondents rated services as more impartial when answering Q10-12 than Q7-9.

Table 4. Equal Treatment in Public Services, Total and by Experience

Country	Education total	experience	no experience	Health Care total	experience	no experience	Law Enforcement total	experience	no experience
1 AT	2.23	2.32	2.13	2.36	2.4	2.25	2.07	2.13	2.04
2 BE	2.27	2.26	2.27	2.04	2.02	2.11	2.43	2.62	2.35
3 BG	2.2	2.15	2.27	2.55	2.53	2.76	2.47	2.54	2.45
4 CZ	2.13	2.09	2.15	2.34	2.34	2.33	2.32	2.5	2.27
5 DE	2.24	2.17	2.29	2.56	2.56	2.54	2.05	2.17	2.01
6 DK	1.96	1.91	1.97	2.01	2.02	1.97	1.77	1.88	1.73
7 ES	2.28	2.23	2.3	2.18	2.18	2.21	2.33	2.5	2.28
8 FI	1.82	1.81	1.83	1.92	1.93	1.92	1.67	1.72	1.65
9 FR	2.41	2.38	2.43	2.4	2.41	2.32	2.62	2.75	2.58
10 GR	2.32	2.13	2.37	2.7	2.71	2.69	2.39	2.37	2.4
11 HR	2.39	2.45	2.35	2.51	2.53	2.33	2.5	2.7	2.41
12 HU	2.01	2.01	2	2.26	2.27	2.24	2.18	2.35	2.15
13 IE	1.75	1.68	1.8	1.96	1.95	1.96	1.85	1.94	1.83
14 IT	2.1	2.08	2.11	2.34	2.35	2.32	2.01	2.07	1.99
15 KO	2.23	2.13	2.3	2.31	2.27	2.36	1.98	2.18	1.94
16 NL	1.79	1.83	1.77	1.56	1.56	1.56	1.81	2	1.75
17 PL	2.18	2.17	2.19	2.63	2.64	2.59	2.25	2.5	2.17
18 PT	2.3	2.32	2.29	2.41	2.41	2.42	2.37	2.48	2.34
19 RO	2.15	2.09	2.18	2.46	2.48	2.41	2.33	2.61	2.26
20 RS	2.7	2.73	2.7	2.82	2.83	2.81	2.74	2.93	2.69
21 SE	2.08	2.09	2.07	2.01	2.01	2.02	1.93	1.93	1.93
22 SK	2.4	2.52	2.31	2.8	2.82	2.71	2.66	2.73	2.63
23 TR	2.21	2.29	2.17	2.09	2.05	2.32	2.16	2.39	2.09
24 UA	2.95	2.92	2.99	3.07	3.1	2.96	3.15	3.31	3.12
25 UK	1.94	1.94	1.94	1.85	1.85	1.84	1.95	2.1	1.91

Note: answer ranges from 1-4, with *lower* numbers equating to greater levels of impartiality.

6. Perceived and experienced corruption in three public services: education, health care and law enforcement.

6.1. Perceived corruption

Q13-15: In this survey we define <u>corruption</u> to mean 'the abuse of entrusted public power for private gain'. This abuse could be by any public employee or politician and the private gain might include money, gifts or other benefits. With this in mind, please respond to the following 3 questions on corruption with a scale of 0-10, with '0' being "strongly disagree" and '10' being "strongly agree"

Q13. "Corruption is prevalent in my area's local public school system"

Q14. "Corruption is prevalent in the public health care system in my area"

Q15. "Corruption is prevalent in the police force in my area"

Table 5. Perceived Corruption in the Public Services

	Education			Health Care			Law Enforcement		
Country	total	experience	no experience	total	experience	no experience	total	experience	no experience
1 AT	3.1	3.26	2.92	3.53	3.62	3.28	2.81	2.6	2.92
2 BE	3.41	3.07	3.59	3.45	3.35	3.76	4.24	4.43	4.16
3 BG	3.41	3.11	3.81	5.49	5.44	5.98	5.06	5.16	5.04
4 CZ	3.34	3.1	3.5	4.29	4.29	4.28	4.22	4.66	4.1
5 DE	2.62	2.49	2.69	3.52	3.56	3.45	2.7	2.69	2.71
6 DK	1.69	1.44	1.79	1.93	1.9	2.09	1.73	1.99	1.66
7 ES	3.55	3.26	3.67	3.85	3.81	4.16	4.12	4.27	4.08
8 FI	1.96	1.7	2.12	2.06	2.05	2.13	1.69	1.51	1.76
9 FR	3.13	2.9	3.32	3.53	3.49	3.76	4.26	4.31	4.25
10 GR	4.09	3.36	4.31	6.16	6.24	6.02	4.83	4.73	4.86
11 HR	4.84	4.54	5.03	5.54	5.65	4.61	5.28	5.39	5.23
12 HU	2.73	2.49	3.04	4.68	4.6	4.96	3.5	3.83	3.44
13 IE	2.05	1.69	2.26	2.12	2.18	1.95	2.22	2.32	2.18
14 IT	3.41	3.14	3.54	4.69	4.71	4.63	3.45	3.55	3.42
15 KO	6	5.36	6.51	6.21	6.21	6.18	4.56	4.95	4.5
16 NL	2.38	2.15	2.5	2.46	2.45	2.5	2.77	3.05	2.69
17 PL	2.29	2.06	2.44	4.18	4.15	4.52	2.97	3.34	2.85
18 PT	4.24	3.94	4.48	4.57	4.56	4.61	4.7	5.09	4.62
19 RO	4.48	4.14	4.63	5.55	5.51	5.68	5	5.56	4.87
20 RS	5.79	5.2	5.96	6.18	6.22	6.01	5.87	6.34	5.76
21 SE	2.74	2.29	2.88	2.71	2.73	2.57	2.46	2.38	2.49
22 SK	4.37	4.43	4.32	5.93	6.01	5.49	5.19	5.25	5.17
23 TR	3.83	4.15	3.67	3.4	3.23	4.24	3.55	4.33	3.29
24 UA	6.17	5.94	6.46	6.69	6.75	6.47	6.95	7.67	6.83
25 UK	2.52	2.26	2.67	2.62	2.57	2.84	2.82	2.99	2.78

Note: answer ranges from 0-10, with *greater* numbers equating to greater levels of corruption.

With a few exceptions, the respondents with direct experience of their area's education and health care services generally perceived them to be less corrupt on the whole than those without any contact over the preceding 12 months. Similarly to the 'quality' questions, the opposite trend can be observed for law enforcement. The gap in perception among people with and without experience is greatest in Ireland, Serbia and Portugal (for education), Croatia, Bulgaria and Slovakia (health care) and Poland, Romania and Ukraine (law enforcement). Yet in most cases, the perception between those with and without direct contact was remarkably similar across countries.

Citizens in Sweden, Denmark and Finland generally rated their three public services in question here as least corrupt, while generally in Ukraine, Serbia and Kosovo the services were thought to be corrupt. In Romania and Bulgaria, health care and law enforcement were seen as corrupt, while in the figures for Greece, health care stands out as particularly problematic.

6.2. Personal Experience of Bribery

Q16. *"In the past 12 months have you or anyone living in your household paid a bribe in any form to"*:

a. *Education services? (yes/ no)*

b. *Health or medical services? (yes/ no)*

c. *Police? (yes/ no)*

d. *Any other government-run agency? (yes/ no)*

The results show that petty corruption in the form of everyday citizens resorting to bribery to gain access to public services in their area occurs on average quite seldom throughout Europe, in particular in education and law enforcement.   Health care is clearly the area in which petty corruption occurs most often in Europe – almost 6% of all respondents reported that they had paid a bribe in the preceding 12 months to obtain some form of health service in their area.   However, the differences between countries are large. For example, in many countries, petty corruption is all but absent from daily life - about 1% or fewer of all respondents from Sweden, UK, Ireland, Denmark, Germany, Spain, Finland, and Netherlands reported paying a bribe over the preceding year for any of the services listed - or for that matter any other public services. However, in certain other countries bribery is much more commonplace, in particular in connection with health care. For example, in eight countries, more than 10% of the respondents had paid a bribe in the health care sector in their area – those countries were Bulgaria, Greece, Hungary, Kosovo, Romania, Slovakia, Italy, and Ukraine and in four of them (Kosovo, Ukraine, Romania and Hungary), more than 20% reported that they had bribed their way to health services. Petty corruption in education over the year preceding the survey had occurred most in Ukraine, Kosovo, Romania and Italy, while for law enforcement about 3% or more of the respondents in Ukraine, Turkey, Romania, Bulgaria and Kosovo reported that they had paid a bribe.

Table 6. Personal Experience with Paying a Bribe

Country	Personal experience with paying a bribe			
	Education	Health care	Law	Other public service
1 AT	0.58	1.72	0	1.72
2 BE	0.41	1.82	1	1.24
3 BG	1.96	15.86	6	2.13
4 CZ	0.59	4.45	1	1.27
5 DE	0.2	0.81	0	0.58
6 DK	0.1	0.1	0	0.05
7 ES	0.26	0.84	0	0.49
8 FI	0.1	0.25	0	0.25
9 FR	0.59	3.07	1	1.68
10 GR	1.05	12.53	1	4.28
11 HR	0.5	7.35	1	1.75
12 HU	0.66	21.23	1	0.91
13 IE	0.13	0.25	0	0.13
14 IT	3.19	11.94	1	3.44
15 KO	5.54	21.05	3	2.78
16 NL	0.52	1.04	0	0.81
17 PL	0.55	6.66	1	1.78
18 PT	0.45	1.6	0	0.35
19 RO	3.88	26.63	3	6.22
20 RS	1.61	9.14	2	3.17
21 SE	0.08	0.54	0	0.15
22 SK	1.62	10.94	2	2.73
23 TR	2.64	1.32	3	1.07
24 UA	11.54	23.08	5	5.5
25 UK	0.29	0.77	1	0.13
total	1.38	5.89	1	1.71

Note: numbers in table are percentages, rounded to nearest hundredth.

The following map in **Figure 5** shows the distribution by region (minus Ukraine, Serbia and Kosovo) of all types of reported petty corruption; the darker the region, the more bribery reported.

Figure 5. Reported Bribery in Europe

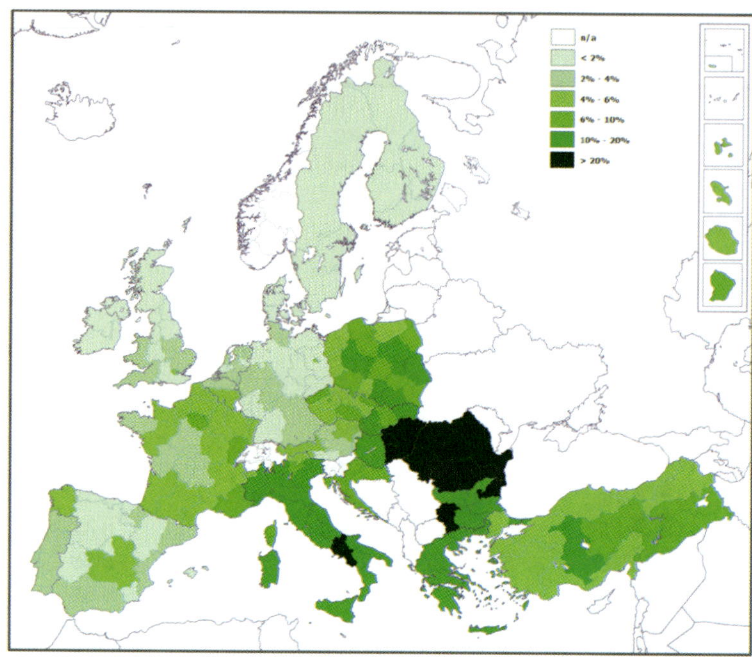

Legend: map reports the percentage of total respondents by region who reported paying a bribe in any of the questions in Q16. Map created by 'Map Generator'.

6.3. Perceived 'Greed Corruption'

Q17: *"In your opinion, how often do you think other people in your area use bribery to obtain other special advantages that they are not entitled to? (0 never - 10 Very frequently)"*

Figure 6. Perceived 'Greed' Corruption

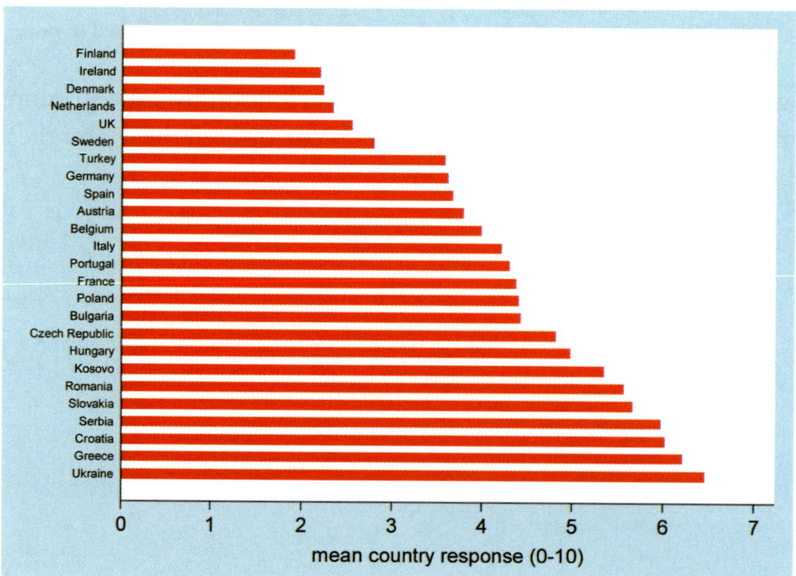

'Greed corruption' is conceived as corruption that occurs 'above' petty corruption so to speak – corruption that occurs for non-essential, publically-funded services such as health care or education.

Most respondents in Ukraine, Greece, Serbia and Kosovo believed that it occurs quite frequently, while in Sweden, Finland, Netherlands, Ireland and Denmark, respondents believed that it seldom occurs.

7. Elections and Media

In the following two questions, respondents were asked about the extent to which corruption is present in their area's elections and their faith in their area's media in reporting corruption in the public sector and among politicians.

Q18-19: Please respond to the following 2 questions with the following ('0' strongly disagree - '10' strongly agree)

Q18: "Elections in my area are clean from corruption"

Figure 7. Perceived Electoral Corruption

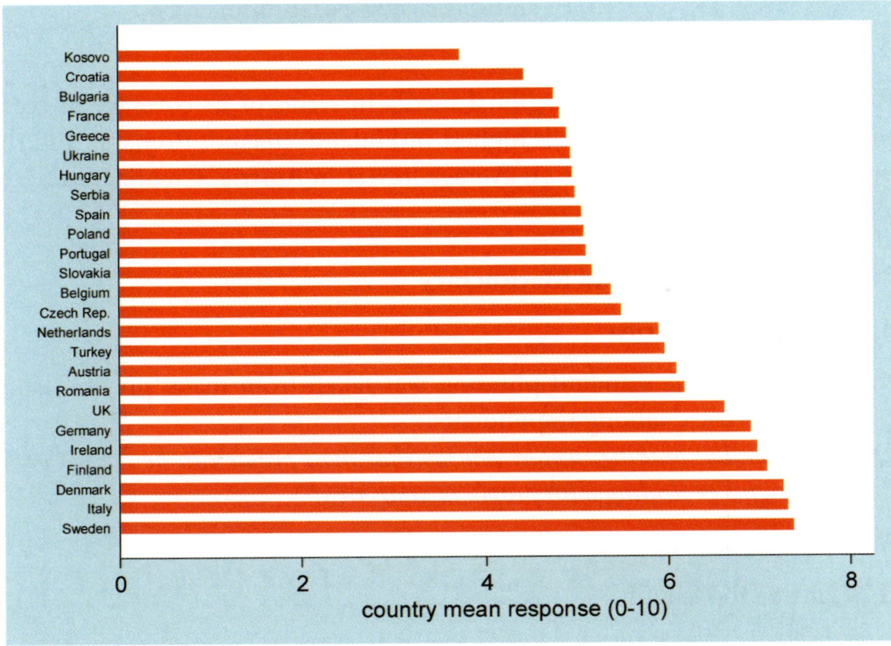

In most cases, the mean response is at or around '5', meaning most believe that elections in their area are moderately free from corruption. Respondents in Sweden, Italy and Denmark rated their elections on average to be quite clean, while in Kosovo and Croatia, a majority rated them as more corrupt than non-corrupt.

Q19: "I trust the information provided by the local mass media on matters of politics and public services in my area".

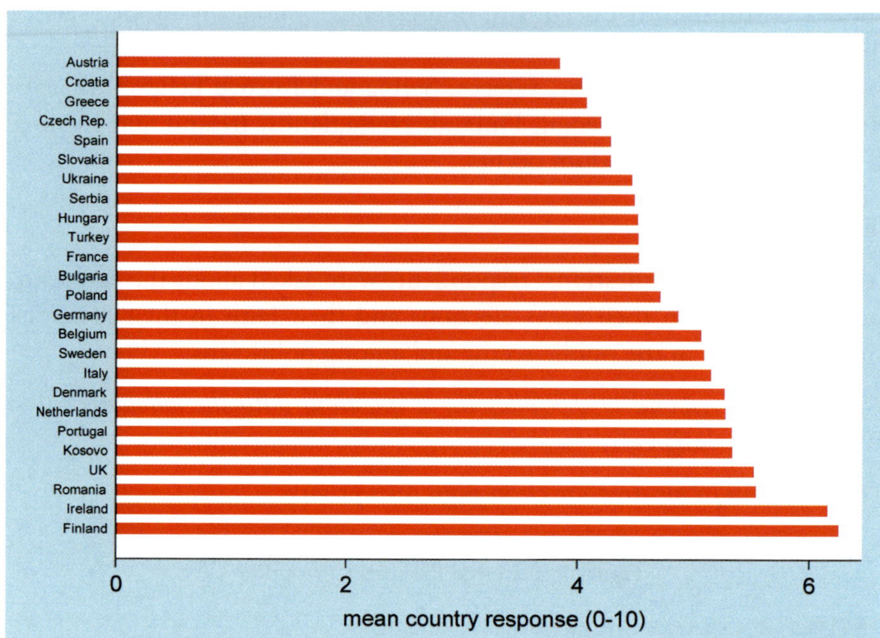

Respondents' trust in their regional media in terms of its coverage of corruption in politics and the public sector is highest in Finland, Ireland, Romania and the U.K. Trust of the local mass media is on average lowest in Austria, Croatia, Greece and the Czech Republic.

8. Questions of Trust and Meritocracy

8.1 Level of social trust

In question 20, the standard phrasing was taken from many previous surveys in capturing 'social trust' among respondents.

Q20: "*Generally speaking, would you say that most people can be trusted or that you can't be too careful in dealing with people in your area?*"

A. "Most people can be trusted"

B. "Can't be too careful"

C. "don't know"

In the aggregate figure, a majority respondents in 10 countries – Germany, Turkey, Austria, Italy, Sweden, the Netherlands, Denmark, the U.K., Finland and Ireland – answered that most people could be trusted. In all the others, a majority responded that one 'can't be too careful'. In several EU countries, the rate of response for 'most people can be trusted' was surprisingly low. In Greece and France it was under 30%, while in Czech Republic and Slovakia, it was fewer than 20%.

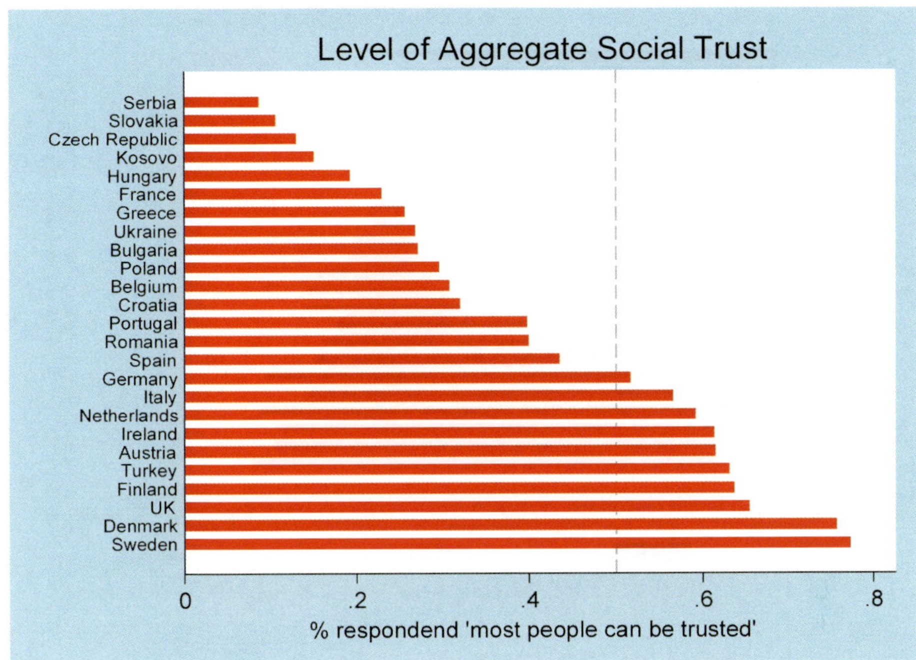

Note: 'don't know' responses not included in calculation. Fewer than 0.5% responded with 'c' however.

8.2. Perceived and experienced level of meritocracy in the public and private sector

Q21: Which statement comes closer to your own views? *'1' means that you agree completely with the statement on the left; '10' means you agree completely with the statement on the right; and if your views fall somewhere in between, you can choose any number in between 1-10.*

8.2.1 Public

Q21a: ("In the public sector most people can succeed if they are willing to work hard") 10 ("Hard work is no guarantee of success in the public sector for most people – *it's more a matter of luck and connections*")

Figure 10 shows two lines for each country – one with the aggregate response of Q21a for all respondents (black) and the other for public sector employees only (red). In all but two cases (Austria and Turkey) public sector workers leaned more towards 'hard work' than 'connections and luck' in their aggregate response. The highest number of public sector workers answering that success in the public sector was meritocratic were found in the UK, Finland and Turkey, while public sector employees in Serbia, Croatia and Slovakia answered that success is driven mostly by connections or luck. The gap in answers between public sector employees and the total response was largest in Greece, Spain, and Bulgaria, and all but negligible in Ukraine, Hungary, Croatia and Austria.

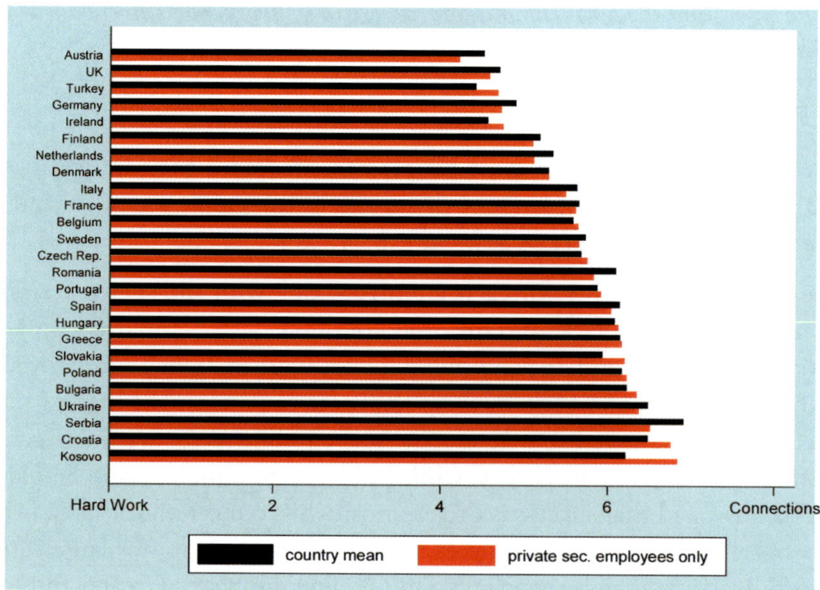

Figure 10. Perceived Merit-Based Public Sector

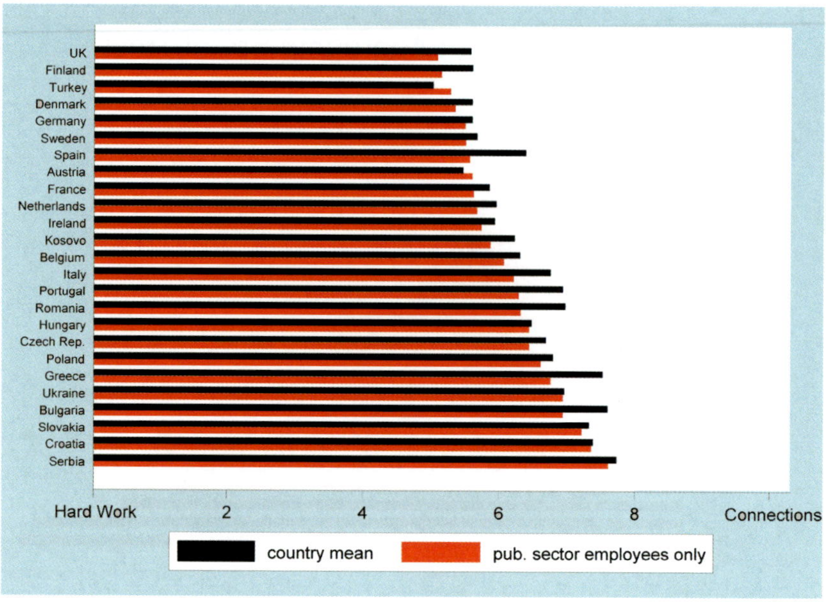

8.2.2 Private

Q21b: ("In business most people can succeed if they are willing to work hard") 10 ("Hard work is no guarantee of success in business for most people – *it's more a matter of luck and connections*")

Figure 11. Perceived Merit-Based Private Sector

Figure 11 shows a similar summary to that in **Figure 10** for meritocracy in the public sector. Among those working in the private sector, respondents from Austria, the U.K. and Turkey found things most meritocratic. Respondents from Kosovo, Croatia, Serbia (minus Kosovo) and Ukraine stated that connections and luck were most important for success in the private sector. The gap between those working in the private sector and the total country response was narrower than for the public sector question (21a), and in several more countries (12 total) respondents actually employed in the private sector rated the private sector as less meritocratic than did the country as a whole. The gap was largest in Kosovo, Serbia, Croatia, Romania and Austria.

9. Political Corruption: Consequences for Political Parties

Q24. *"What political party would you vote for if the national parliamentary election were today?"*

While most questions in this survey focused on perceptions and experience with regional services, these questions asked respondents about voting patterns at national level. For this question, respondents were read a pre-coded list of all actual political parties, including the category "other". The lists included all political parties that polled above their respective country's electoral threshold from the previous election, or any new party above that threshold which was standing in an election in the coming year (for example, the Italian party '5 Stelle'). All voters were then asked to name one party. Those results can be obtained via the individual levels survey data.

Question 25 deals then with the consequences for future voting of an imagined corruption scandal.

Q25. *"Now imagine that that party was involved in a corruption scandal, which of the following would be most likely?"*
  1. Still vote for preferred party
  2. Vote for another established party not involved in the corruption scandal
  3. Not vote at all
On average, about 21% of all respondents stated that even if their preferred party were to be involved in a corruption scandal they would continue to vote for that party in a forthcoming election. About 34% and 39% respectively said that they would either vote for another established party or simply not vote at all. Roughly 7% of the respondents gave no answer.

For Q25, there were significant differences among countries in the aggregate responses. Respondents in Turkey, Czech Republic, Germany and Romania were most likely to say they would be inclined to continue to vote for their preferred party irrespective of any corruption scandal, while those in Greece, Serbia and Portugal were by far the least inclined to do so. The majority of respondents from Denmark, the Netherlands and Sweden said they would vote for another established party, while the majority of respondents in Spain, France, Portugal and Serbia would simply stay at home and not vote at all.

Table 7. Voting Intentions for Corrupt Parties

	Country	Still Vote	e Another P:	Not Vote	n/a
1	AT	24.9	40.9	26.8	7.4
2	BE	19.8	41.1	37.2	2
3	BG	19	25.8	37.5	18
4	CZ	28.1	32	35	5
5	DE	27.4	32.8	30.1	9.6
6	DK	21.9	55.7	14	8.4
7	ES	10.1	33.4	52.3	4.2
8	FI	24.3	41.6	27.8	6.4
9	FR	24.2	19.5	53.8	2.5
10	GR	5	49.3	44.3	1.4
11	HR	13.7	36.3	44.2	5.8
12	HU	25.7	22.6	46.2	5.5
13	IE	16.9	46.5	32.9	3.8
14	IT	19.6	36.5	37.5	6.4
15	KO	11.3	23.8	45.5	20
16	NL	15.9	57.5	17.9	8.7
17	PL	13.9	29.5	45.1	12
18	PT	9.9	27.8	50.5	12
19	RO	26.5	26.3	46.9	0.3
20	RS	6	18.4	56.7	19
21	SE	25.9	50.1	18.6	5.4
22	SK	18.6	37.6	39.4	4.4
23	TR	35.5	37.1	24.1	3.3
24	UA	26	20.3	32.1	22
25	UK	23.3	34.4	38.2	4.1
total		20.8	33.7	38.6	6.9

Sources

Charron, Nicholas, Lewis Dijkstra & Victor Lapuente 2013. 'Regional Governance Matters: Quality of Government within European Union Member States', *Regional Studies*, DOI:1 0.1080/00343404.2013.770141

Charron, Nicholas, Victor Lapuente & Bo Rothstein 2013. 'Quality of Government and Corruption from a European Perspective'. Edward Elgar Publishing.

Charron, Nicholas, Victor Lapuente & Bo Rothstein 2010. "Measuring the Quality of Government in the EU and Sub-national Variation", Report for the *European Commission* Directorate-General Regional Policy and Directorate Policy Development, 2010

Kaufmann, Daniel, Aart Kraay & Massimo Mastruzzi 2010. 'The Worldwide Governance Indicators: Methodology and Analytical Issues.' *World Bank Policy Research Working Paper*, No. 5430.

Tabellini, Guido 2005. "Culture and Institutions: Economic Development in the Regions of Europe" *IGIER Working Paper* No. 292. Available at SSRN: http://ssrn.com/abstract=754086

Transparency International 2012. *Corruption Perceptions Index.* Available at: http://cpi.transparency.org/cpi2012/

9. Lessons learned. The Good, the Bad and the Ugly

ALINA MUNGIU-PIPPIDI

This policy report reviews the lessons learned from the three European political regions researched by ANTICORRP in the first year of the project: the EU, the South-Eastern Europe and the Former Soviet Union (FSU). Given the large differences among countries, recommendations are different for the three European regions, and are based on the corruption model presented in these regional reports, as well as on the more specific policy data presented in the Romanian, Estonian and Hungarian case studies.

The Anticorruption Report 1 offers these five contributions to the objectives of the project:

I. On defining corruption

One main finding arising from this report arising from this report is the important presence of 'legal corruption', including favouritism of businesses by government, preferential allocation of public funds and more generally favouritism in public services and law enforcement. According to the ANTICORRP pan-European survey reported in this volume by Nicholas Charron, favouritism is more widespread than previously thought and accounts for most of what European citizens call corruption. Favouritism plays an important role in deterring economic performance, and it subverts political legitimacy and trust. This report shows that this type of corruption is present in a large number of countries and is not limited to those that are usually considered corrupt or suffer from visible corruption scandals. While the countries where the survey shows favouritism of public services as most problematic are not EU members (e.g. Serbia, Ukraine), the case studies from Hungary and Romania show that favouritism and discretionary allocation of public resources are also major issues in some EU member countries. This is particularly evident in the realm of public fiscal management, which is usually the one citizens know the least about.

II. On producing new, change sensitive corruption indicators which are not perception based.

This report offers two types of new indicators. **The first are pure policy indicators** and come from the Romanian and Hungarian examples (presented in the comparative report, as well as in the two case studies). The methodology for computing these indicators is similar for all the examples provided in this report and consists of a survey of public resources allocation (funds or contracts of public procurement) followed by an analysis of the result's distribution or a comparison with a benchmark category. When the results show a distribution that is far from random or is statistically implausible, they hint at a hidden organizing factor, i.e. corruption. In Romania, for instance, mayors who belong to the government parties are disproportionately benefitting from funds for natural emergencies, and this disparity has been growing from one electoral cycle to another. Romanian companies with political ties also win more public contracts than internationally reputed firms and make huge profits even in times of crisis. In the case of Hungary, the turnover and profit of politically connected companies is simply reversed when the winner of elections changes. These examples come from countries where ANTICORRP researchers were more advanced in collecting data and should not be seen as exceptional. Similar studies should be undertaken in Italy, Slovakia, Greece and a score of other countries to check on such indicators since this type of government favouritism causes important market distortions.

The second category of indicators developed by the project is made of determinants of corruption. Due to an explanatory model based only on policy and not on structural factors, we are able to significantly attribute corruption to human agency as manifested in policies or different institutional arrangements. We know, for example, that red tape is bad for corruption because it has a statistically significant association with the aggregated corruption rankings computed by the World Bank and Transparency International. As shown in this report, these corruption indicators show a remarkable consistency between them, which suggests that, despite being based on perceptions, they point to a similar reality. We therefore believe that monitoring a country on determinants of corruption, once the statistical model is proven robust, can bring great policy benefit, as most of them can be changed by human action. Testing other indicators and policies remains a main goal of ANTICORRP as this opens the door to a permanent assessment of anticorruption policies' impact.

III. On identifying corruption and anticorruption risks

Using the methodology described above, this report establishes policy based risk categories where countries are ranked according to their performance on various objective policy indicators (i.e. not perception-based indicators). The indicators used to construct the ranking were identified as significant determinants of corruption. A further method to categorize countries according to their corruption risks was developed in the comparative report on South-Eastern Europe (Chapter 3). In that section, corruption and anticorruption risks were combined for the first time to create an indicator of **implementation gap**. We argue that policies designed to improve governance and policies not directly related to corruption, have the potential of increasing corruption as an unintended consequence since they risk widening the gap between law and practice. Therefore, enforcement will and implementation capacity are major factors to account for when selecting an anticorruption policy. We further argue that whenever a country deals with some degree of group or party capture of the state, grounding anticorruption policies in the government alone is counter-productive and will increase the risks of corruption instead of decreasing them.

IV. On the highest risk and greatest achievement

The report identifies Bulgaria, Czech Republic, Greece, Latvia, Poland and Romania as facing the highest corruption risks in the European Union, with a more problematic situation than previously thought also for Slovakia, Slovenia, Italy, Portugal and Spain. The process of EU integration does not improve governance by itself. Greece and Italy, for example, have regressed instead of progressed since their accession to the EU. Moreover, the new member countries only showed some progress before accession, but they have regressed since. The shining exception is Estonia but, as the case study shows, progress in this country is due to a political dynamic of its own reforms and not due to EU conditionality. Estonian continuity in government of parties which have drastically curtailed discretionary spending and increased administrative transparency has worked: **The country presents the greatest global progress in controlling corruption by reducing opportunities for corrupt behaviour.** The Estonian lessons are applicable elsewhere and should be replicated whenever possible. The downside is, of course, that such political elites enjoying this kind of support are not easy to find, but their policies could and should be transferred whoever international donors and EU have a say.

V. On the economic crisis and effect on the free market

The primary and secondary data analysed by ANTICORRP shows that the dramatic **consequences of corruption are a major impediment to economic recovery in the EU.** Corruption **bolsters deficits on behalf of discretionary spending (and hurts investment in public health and education), reduces tax collection, detriments the absorption rate of EU funds, and further generates vulnerable employment and brain drain.** Fundamentally, as data from the less developed part of Europe (but also Hungary) shows, **corruption affects free market competition. Both, domestic markets and global competition are affected by government favouritism and vested interests in certain companies. As a result, bribery needs to be seen as a part of this larger picture of market distortion and as a way to open an otherwise preferential market. Therefore, criminalizing only bribery and not all forms of market favouritism does not have much potential to correct the distortion.**

It is not the aim of this report to make recommendations for individual countries beyond the general analytical framework laid out here, but that framework is essential. Since those factors differ greatly, however, recommendations are grouped into ten generic categories:

> ### 1. *Effective anticorruption policies are broad good governance policies not based solely on repression.*

> Even when we manage to document anticorruption policies at the European and global level, control of corruption as equilibrium is influenced by so many powerful factors that even effective policies do not manage to account for much difference across countries. Only countries which are more transparent fare

significantly better in controlling corruption. **Countries which have a specialized anticorruption agency or have adopted more legislation do not perform better**. Repressive policies alone do not seem to work where corruption is a major problem. Anticorruption has to be understood in a broader governance context and policies to reduce or at least not increase opportunities and resources for corruption (as is the case with EU funds) need to be promoted.

2. There are serious limitations of international approaches to national anticorruption which should be considered at all times.

Recently, the European Union has been very active and plans to be even more so in pursuing cross-border anticorruption activities and promoting global legislation against tax havens, money laundering and assets' recovery. These policies are extremely valid, but some limitations apply which should be considered at all times. First, expectations tied to such policies should be moderate. Evidence shows that control of corruption is a national equilibrium. Unless it is seriously affected at its origin, tax evasion and other behaviours of this type will reproduce themselves. In other words, we should not expect policies which cut the dragon's head to be sustainable if dragons are known to grow three heads for each one cut off. Such policies do not touch the underlying causes of corruption. Asset recovery, for example, is extraordinarily costly and will not be cost effective if applied in isolation from a serious attempt to shake the vicious equilibrium in the country where the assets were originally stolen. These policies also risk increasing red tape in countries which fall below the 65 percentile in the World Bank control of corruption rankings (which is closely correlated with rule of law) thus generating more corruption instead of reducing it. Therefore, unintended consequences should be very carefully weighted, bearing in mind that whenever rule of law is still problematic, tighter laws will create a larger implementation gap and not solve problems. Only a combination of policies addressing causes and result-tracing can hope to produce some lasting and sustainable success.

3. Policies which do not pass a cost-effective examination, either due to very high costs (including political), or proven lack of impact should be discarded.

The current generation of anticorruption policies has been promoted with little or no cost-effectiveness analysis, despite evidence that impact is quite impossible to prove. We have meanwhile developed new indicators allowing the tracking of progress by sectors or over time. In the future, policies should be more evidence based. The Romanian example on competition in the infrastructure sector is telling: such indicators are needed to understand and prevent government favouritism, the most harmful form of corruption for the common market.

4. Reducing administrative opportunities for corruption is essential.

Such reforms are indispensable for nearly all Mediterranean and East European countries. Rather than presuming with no evidence that those countries need special anticorruption units or new legislation, there is evidence that they can easily obtain more effective results if they focus on administrative reforms, cut red tape, liberalize trade, streamline regulation to reduce informality, increase transparency (in particular fiscal transparency to allow monitoring of government expenses in real time through online tracking systems, but also transparency allowing monitoring of politicians and policymaking) and develop e-government. These measures would work especially well for countries such as Italy, Greece, Cyprus, Slovakia, the Czech Republic, Poland, Lithuania, Malta, Spain and Romania. Countries like Latvia, Estonia and even Bulgaria have already undertaken reform to become more 'Scandinavian' and it is the right way for them to go, although great challenges remain. East European countries have the shining examples of Estonia and Georgia to follow.

5. Reducing fiscal opportunities for corruption plays a very large role and austerity can help anticorruption if it is exercised on behalf of discretionary (government investment) and not universalistic spending (education).

This report brings ample evidence that government investment is feeding corruption far more than economic recovery. Discretionary spending is a major source of legal corruption and subverts sound public finances, competiveness and growth. Good spending is universalistic spending with a clear destination, for instance education and health. Bad public spending is any spending where discretion is high. Spending on new infrastructure projects, for example, allows to channel government resources to favourite companies either directly or through local or regional governments, producing unnecessary outputs with high costs. Apart from fiscal transparency, which is indispensable for good governance, it is recommended that the structure of public expenses channels resources to education, skill development, research, innovation and public health in countries where our survey shows that **gifts from patients are a major source of public health financing. Governments should instead manifest austerity in all other forms of public investment.**

6. The auditing mechanisms of EU funds should be refined and connected to an impact evaluation of funds

The report also argues that EU funds for countries with poor control of corruption only manage to further feed local client-driven spending in the absence of an early warning mechanism based on social accountability. It also brings evidence that corruption subverts absorption of EU funds and thus economic recovery of countries which are already the poorest in EU. The solution recommended is the development of a link between the EU evaluation of the opportunity and impact of such funds, in cooperation with regional civil society and business, on the one hand, and the oversight and audit mechanisms on the other. Presently the control mechanism of EU funds is purely bureaucratic (it is not checked if building of a soccer stadium is indeed the proper investment for tourism infrastructure in a city where tourists come only during the soccer league break) and top down. It has also developed in the last years, when confronted with unprecedented corruption, a repressive approach, suspending all funds at the warning of irregularities. The report argues that this further diminishes the chances of economic recovery of poor countries and that a more specific mechanism can be created to protect funds better without hurting absorption.

7. Public audit capacity should be increased in unconventional forms, for instance by cooperation with the private and third sector.

This applies especially to Italy, Bulgaria, Latvia, Spain and Greece, but also to a lesser extent to all post-communist countries and should be seen as part of administrative reform. It can also be treated more creatively, by introducing audits by private sector, civil society, stakeholders, or combinations of the above. Such creative state-society approaches to audit are especially needed in countries of Eastern Europe and the Balkans, where evidence exists that control agencies sometimes engage in extortion and discretional enforcement.

8. Judicial autonomy and accountability should be permanently and publicly monitored.

The judicial autonomy from power and its accountability when corruption is concerned remain serious problems in some East European countries and in South Eastern Europe. But more work needs being done also in Romania, Italy, Greece, Bulgaria, the Slovak Republic, and, to a lesser extent, in Latvia, Lithuania, Spain and the Czech Republic. This is obviously more of a goal than an action itself, so it should not be itself the centrepiece of any anticorruption strategy. Italy has relied on this strategy alone in the last twenty years with some notorious successful prosecutions, but an overall small progress. Countries should self-organize their judiciaries as they see fit, as no design is ideal, but their performance should be the object of permanent monitoring and public debate.

9. National civil society capability for monitoring governance and controlling corruption at both national and local levels should be increased and applied to EU cohesion and assistance funds in particular.

The existence of watchful and demanding citizens is an essential deterrent for the rent seeking behaviour of governments. Evidence shows an insufficient level of societal constraints to corrupt behaviour across nearly all Eastern Europe (Ukraine struggles, with wide internal differences) and the Balkans. In the EU alone, this applies to Romania, Portugal, Greece, Slovakia, Poland, Cyprus, Bulgaria, Latvia, Spain and Slovenia. Policies to increase civil society oversight capacity include

- systems of social accountability designed for the auditing of public expenses or budget planning (with civil society and business groups being permanently involved in the monitoring of EU funds and other government expenses, for instance);
- support from government to develop broad internet access and use, especially at local community level. Even the smallest village becomes capable to improve its governance if it has one Internet café where locals can gather to monitor town hall expenses, fill online petitions or read the statements of assets of the judge presiding their land trial;

- development of civil society, on the model of assistance programmes to developing countries, especially in less developed contexts where the number of people involved in civil society groups is very small.

Unfortunately, this policy has serious limitations. Some countries like Russia do not encourage anticorruption grassroots activity and even repress funding of such organizations. Anticorruption is seen as politically subversive by authoritarian governments and anticorruption NGOs are at risk in many East European countries. In Georgia, Ukraine, Moldova and Armenia the situation is somewhat better, but civil society still faces considerable challenges even there. In the Balkans, EU accession offers more incentives and resources to civil society anticorruption activities, but they remain seriously insufficient in Albania, Bosnia, Macedonia and Montenegro.

The situation is particularly poor in some new EU member countries. With the exception of Estonia, no new EU member country has an operational program dedicated to civil society and the EU funds for building oversight capacity of civil society are practically zero. In countries like Czech Republic, Slovakia, Romania and Bulgaria the grassroots fight against corruption exists based on only a handful of activists. If only a tiny fraction of the EU funds intended for projects in Sicily or Bulgaria went to citizens' associations that could take part in the planning, evaluation and auditing of such projects, and if all the expenses could be published in real time on the Internet, an immediate improvement would be felt. Thirty years of EU evaluations have not managed to uncover what any Sicilian villager could have told evaluators from the onset: what is the money really for (or whom) and how it was really spent, because such evaluations never consult the villagers. The empowerment of those who lose from corruption is the most neglected from all the potentially effective and sustainable anticorruption strategies.

10. An economically depressed media faces high risk of capture and needs support to be able to enforce its role as good governance watchdog.

All across Europe mass media suffers from various degrees of vested interests capture in this difficult economic environment and thus becomes less and less able to play the main role they could in building control of corruption. A media outlet in the hands of a corrupt politician or an oligarch whose private fortune is built on capturing public funds will not do its civic job to report and investigate corruption and protect public interest through accurate reporting. Governments who want to help, and not control media, and the international community should promote increased transparency of media ownership and advertising revenues to protect media from capture by vested interests in difficult economic environments. EU funds should also support new media and civil society organizations acting as watchdogs and contributing to an increase in the public awareness of government and officials' expenses in member states, associated states and neighbourhood countries.

Acknowledgments

The present policy report: **The Anticorruption Report 1: Controlling Corruption in Europe** is the first volume of the policy series **"The Anti-Corruption Report"** produced in the framework of EU FP7 ANTICORRP Project. The report was edited by Prof. Dr. Alina Mungiu-Pippidi from Hertie School of Governance, head of the policy pillar of the project.

ANTICORRP is a large-scale research project funded by the European Commission's Seventh Framework Programme. The full name of the project is "Anti-corruption Policies Revisited: Global Trends and European Responses to the Challenge of Corruption". The project started in March 2012 and will last for five years. The research is conducted by 21 research groups in sixteen countries.

The fundamental purpose of ANTICORRP is to investigate and explain the factors that promote or hinder the development of effective anti-corruption policies and impartial government institutions. A central issue is how policy responses can be tailored to deal effectively with various forms of corruption. Through this approach ANTICORRP seeks to advance the knowledge on how corruption can be curbed in Europe and elsewhere. Special emphasis is laid on the agency of different state and non-state actors to contribute to building good governance.

Project acronym: ANTICORRP
Project full title: Anti-corruption Policies Revisited: Global Trends and European Responses to the Challenge of Corruption
Project duration: March 2012 – February 2017
EU funding: Approx. 8 million Euros
Theme: FP7-SSH.2011.5.1-1
Grant agreement number: 290529
Project website: http://anticorrp.eu/

Due to the number and density of the annexes and references to sources we had to exclude many of them from the print version of this policy publication. The online versions of print-shortened chapters (2, 4, 6, 7, 8) including all the annexes and full references are available at http://anticorrp.eu/ and www.againstcorruption.eu.